Inkslingers 2013:

Memoirs of the Southwest

Inkslingers 2013:

Memoirs of the Southwest

Eveline Horelle Dailey,
Executive Editor

Two Cats Press
Surprise, AZ

Two Cats Press
17608 W. Columbine Drive, Surprise, AZ 85388

Executive Editor: Eveline Horelle Dailey
Managing Editor: Ekta Garg

ISBN-13: 978-1-937083-33-5
ISBN-10: 1-937083-33-0

The authors have made every effort to ensure the accuracy and completeness of the writing contained in this book.

Cover design by Christopher Wilke.
Design and typesetting by Gale Leach.

Printed in the U.S.A.

Contents

Foreword   vii   Bob Duckles

Acknowledgements   ix   Eveline Horelle Dailey

Executive Editor's Note   x   Eveline Horelle Dailey

A Note from the Managing Editor   xi   Ekta Garg

---

50 Miles to Phoenix   3   Vincent A. Alascia

Thorns   7   Vincent A. Alascia

Finally Getting to Say Goodbye   12   Helene Benigno-Stich

Grandfather and the Saguaro   19   Jen Bielack

Oak Creek Rising   24   Jen Bielack

Betrayal and Hope in the Desert   29   Carmela Ayello Bottita

It's a Dry Heat   34   Donna Bowring

Too Soon   41   Donna Bowring

The Road Less Taken:
Our Journey to Ghost Ranch   43   Ellen Buikema

Go Farther, Go Faster   49   Heather Cappel

A Book Cover   55   Eveline Horelle Dailey

I Met A Master   59   Eveline Horelle Dailey

The Inipe   64   Eveline Horelle Dailey

In the Presence of Royalty: A Memoir   71   John Daleiden
Boundaries   72
On Your Wedding Day   74
The Healing   75
. . . As Time Goes By . . .   75
While We Wait   76
Caught in the Path   77
In the Valley of the Sun   79
In the Stillness at Sunrise   81

Failure of the Heart in the Valley of the Sun	83	Bob Duckles
You'll Never Forget Your First	89	Matt Estrada
Desert Oasis	94	Colleen Grady
Making Friends in Arizona	102	Dawn Gunn
Rethinking Life's Truths	106	Donna Hamill
Sharing Sweat in Arizona	111	Donna Hamill
The Telephone	116	Elizabeth Kral
Grandpa's Arizona Family	123	Gale Leach
The Shooting Match	130	Gale Leach
The Wrong-Way Quail	138	Gale Leach
Thirst	144	Justin Loyd
Browned Flour	151	Jessie Swierski
Arizona Blue	154	Jessie Swierski
The Curse of Wide Ruins Trading Post	159	Janice M. Toland
Dying on Sandia Peak	166	Janice M. Toland
The Mystery of the Jerome Grand Hotel	173	Janice M. Toland
The Window Screen War	179	Janice M. Toland
My Kind of Place	186	Rita Toma
Safe Is a Mirage	191	Rachel Wallis
You Asked About My First Love	198	Rachel Wallis
Follow the Sun	205	Dori Williams

⌐◦⌐

Biographies	213	

Foreword

Since its beginning six years ago, the West Valley Writer's Workshop has focused on getting writers published and, once published, getting read. Presenters to the workshop have provided valuable information on how and why to create a platform; successfully pitching our writing to agents and editors; and strategizing to get our work before the reader. We have always devoted less time to providing critical feedback on original writing than most other writing groups.

In the early days, when 12 to 18 members would attend the meetings, we would kick around the idea of creating an anthology. This would give writers a platform as published authors. We even collected a few submissions but had trouble moving the project forward, in part because we only had a few submissions.

The Workshop grew. More than 100 members enrolled on our website, and our meetings regularly had 20 to 25 members in attendance. We developed some real energy around publishing an anthology, and we began to see evidence of more people willing to provide their work. In 2012 Eveline Horelle Dailey accepted the challenge of being the first anthology's executive editor. Beyond that, she persevered and saw the project to completion. Without her pushing, gentle pleading, defining deadlines, making tough decisions, wonderful good humor, and surviving moments that could have driven normal people to despair, *Avondale Inkslingers: An Anthology* would never have become a reality.

Even more amazingly Eveline offered to turn around and do it again this year, only bigger and better. The members of the Workshop who attended meetings early this year came to a consensus that this time we wanted an anthology of memoirs, with the Southwest as a unifying theme.

Twenty-two authors have written about their experiences moving into, in, around, through, and away from the Valley of the Sun and other Southwestern spots. They touch on life and death; celebrating and mourning. We read of tears and laughter. We participate in journeys of planting, growing, nurturing, and harvesting. We meet the stranger. We meet the familiar—sometimes family—with various mixtures of love, sorrow, pain, and delight. We learn of longing, separation, and belonging. These writers lead us through dreams and nightmares, stumbles and recoveries. We meet bright angels and dark demons in backyards and wild places.

These are rich experiences to be savored. This book is no mere vanity collection. It contains the full process of being a real author: doing the solitary work of stitching together stories, having your work selected (not every submission made the cut), then going through a thorough editing process with our professional editor, Ekta Garg. We have learned about deadlines and formatting requirements. Not only will these authors see their work printed and bound into a book, they will participate in a group process to making their work known with a launch party to attract readers. This is very much a workshop project to hone all the crafts involved in becoming an author who people will read.

The product is a collection of gems told from real life experiences, offered to us with real talent and skill. Thanks to all the authors, and a very special thanks to Eveline Horelle Dailey without whom this project would still be a dream.

Bob Duckles
West Valley Writer's Workshop Organizer
September 2013

Acknowledgements

We must take a moment to thank the entire staff and particularly Ava Gutwein of the Avondale Library for allowing us the space to grow from. This anthology is a direct response of our gratitude.

Christopher Wilke, knowing a book without a cover was a personality without a face, used his talent and created for us a cover that shows well who we are. The Inkslingers thank you, Chris!

The words and sentences written here are akin to an edible garden—many colors, many flavors blended by the writers of this anthology. I congratulate and give a standing ovation to each of them.

Once penned, the writer's words become a work of art only after the editor polishes it. We thank Ekta Garg for working with us.

Nothing is a book until it has been formatted to look like a book to be a book. Gale Leach of Two Cats Press used her talent and technology to bring forth this tome. We could not have published it without her. We owe her a debt of gratitude.

Ultimately, none of the above would be necessary without the leadership, encouragement and guidance of Bob Duckles, our leader in matters of the West Valley Writers Workshop. With sure and subtle hands he guided each of us. Now, as authors, we thank him.

Eveline Horelle Dailey

Executive Editor's Note

My engagement with this year's publication of the InkSlingers 2013 Anthology was an honor I had not anticipated. I was to be the keeper of a well-guarded gate while an anonymous reader decided who would be accepted and who would not.

One day, I opened the sacred gate, penetrated a corridor lit with the jewels of the old, I entered a room. A chair, a table and pages floated toward me—I began to read.

Knowing that most successful writers spend years writing and improving their craft I soon became aware that at my fingertip I had the works of successful of men and women who had gained mastery of their craft.

I understood the honor granted me, I felt awed and privileged.

I had read the virgin works of authors where each word was positioned perfectly where it would do the maximum good to advance the most varied memoirs. My gluttony gave way to the expression you hold today.

Each work in this book is brought to the reader by a level-headed and surefooted author.

I am certain, in the not too distinct future, I will say, I knew him or her when….

Eveline Horelle Dailey

A Note from the Managing Editor

When executive editor Eveline Horelle Dailey approached me last year to act as managing editor (ME) of the first Avondale Inkslingers anthology, I felt excited. I knew she had given me an opportunity that would challenge and invigorate me. When I found out I had to edit the work of almost two dozen writers, I drew a deep breath and let it out slowly. What, I thought, had I gotten myself into? Could I fulfill this role? Would I do justice to the confidence Eveline had shown by choosing me?

Most importantly: how would I keep track of everyone?

At the end of the five weeks of editing the anthology, I knew the answers. I had gotten myself into an amazing prospect to learn from and work with some incredibly talented people. Even though I felt scattered at some point, yes, I could actually act as the ME for this project. With regards to the question of Eveline's confidence, either I fooled her well enough or she is an incredibly forgiving person: she asked me to come back as ME again this year.

And Microsoft Excel can do wonders for keeping track of people.

For me the biggest advantage came in the answer to the first question. I got to read pieces that made me laugh out loud, gasp in surprise, or keep me quiet as I pondered the thought-provoking premise of a story. More than anything, I had an absolute blast. Despite the "editing blizzard," as I've come to call it, I didn't even blink when Eveline asked me back.

This year the Avondale Inkslingers chose the Southwest as the theme of the anthology, an apt pick given the location of the group. But choosing a theme so close to home—literally—might have put off some readers. People in Pittsburgh or Tampa or

Sacramento might ask themselves, why should they spend their time reading this book?

Because these stories, while set in and around the Southwest, do what stories do best: they transcend any boundaries and reach deep into the hearts of all of us as humans. Love; betrayal; joy; grief. People across the country and even the world share these emotions and so many more, and readers can find exactly that in this book: the common experience.

Readers of this anthology will receive an immense gift by encountering works by some seasoned writers. But the West Valley Writers Workshop also encourages and invites those new to the craft to delve into themselves and draw out stories. With that in mind, Eveline and I chose one piece that we feel exemplifies the anthology's theme and also shows a great deal of potential for future work.

With great pleasure we name Justin Loyd, author of the story "Thirst," with the inaugural recognition of "Editors' Choice for New Talent." Justin's story will draw in readers with its inventive prose and aching reality. Its universal theme and ending will surely cause readers to agree that Justin stands at the beginning of a promising writing career.

Both Eveline and I would like to thank all of the writers for their hard work and patience throughout the editing process. We congratulate all of them on their success in inclusion in this anthology, and we look forward to sharing more stories with readers in the future.

Ekta Garg, managing editor
The Write Edge
Thewriteedge.wordpress.com

The Stories

50 Miles to Phoenix

Vincent A. Alascia

Janis Joplin's voice rang out from my car's speakers singing about freedom being just another word. The highway rolled past, and the sun hung in the sky like a golden tack pressed into a veil of blue satin that held back the empty darkness of space. The road ahead shone and simmered with promise and very little in the way of absolutes. Would anyone expect it differently? The safe ones would.

The safe ones: those who seek comfort in what they can see and touch, control and expect. To them the open road is treacherous and a courting of disaster. I used to be one of the safe ones. I would measure every inch twice and cut just once. That may have given me the perfect bookshelf but very little to place on it. Change called to me and my wife, tempted, begged and at last ushered in a new phase of our life. I was now fifty miles from Phoenix in the state of Arizona, our new home.

Moving is always a lot more than packing a truck. Planning how to move with my wife and two felines took longer than the decision itself. Yet, as if the universe approved, all of the details fell into place. We both managed to land new jobs within a few days of each other; apparently librarians who know their way around a computer screen are still in demand. Our current house in Delaware sold after only six days on the market. We even managed to get ourselves an apartment with just days to go before the moving van would leave with all our stuff.

The house in Dover was my first home, so leaving it was a little harder than expected. Or maybe that was just the part of my brain that fought back against all the change. No, it was some emotional stuff too. I drained the spa for the last time and took a walk around the gardens we had planted. That all left me by the time I reached the middle of the Bay Bridge on our way to Pennsylvania for the first leg of the drive.

As a child I often only saw what I could not do. Freedom appeared as distant as that horizon out in front of the speeding bumper of my car. As children we are spared the knowledge that freedom is just consequence in disguise. You could lie in bed and wonder if the monster beneath your bed means you harm, or you could lean over the side and check. If the monster was hungry you got eaten, but at least you no longer had to worry. You exercised your freedom, as did the monster.

The highway goes both forward and back at the same time, depending on the window you look out. I looked out the front window as the pine trees gave way to cacti. Occasionally I looked in the rear view mirror, but I knew what was back there was only a reflection.

A cross country drive frees you up to think. I was alone in the car, so I had all my thoughts to myself. The original plan was to split up our two cats. Mina would ride with my wife and mother-in-law while Morgan, "the noisy one," would ride with me. That plan kind of fell through once we discussed the logistics of eating and bathroom breaks. While holding my pee for eight hours would not be impossible, there are other *movements* that are less compliant to human will. The thought of leaving a cat alone in her cage, albeit locked in a car that also contained my guitars and amplifier, was not very comfortable, so the trip necessitated that both felines would ride with my wife and mother-in-law who could better split up bathroom and watching duties.

While I missed the companionship, I did get to pore over all the decisions that led up to this move. Sometimes, in an odd twist, the fear is not over what may come but over what we may have left behind. Indecision only worsens after the decision is made. Hoping for an ace after the deck has been cleared from the table is useless, but we do it anyway. When you think of all the decisions you make, the simple ones are easy to spot: a Milky Way or a Snickers Bar, McDonalds or Burger King, sleep or another hour of playing Halo.

Then there are the decisions made for us, or made in such a way as to hide our choices, that never leave us content. We relish the thought that if we follow our hearts all will be well. I was following my heart into the desert, but more than that I *chose* to follow my heart into the desert. I had had enough of the choices that common sense rejected or that my ego whispered me out of.

These decisions haunted me enough and ate tiny wormholes in the otherwise-firm foundation of my past. This was not going to be one of those decisions. Events happen, but actions occur. The hero dies whether he chooses to take up the sword or not. The hero lives when he strikes with the sword. Attack the future. Never let a dream pass with the sunrise—that was my new mantra.

The air inside the car mingled with some dust from outside, flavored by the aroma of French fries long since devoured. The dashboard gave off a heat to rival the asphalt beneath the tires. The radio played on. I love it when driving requires little in the form of concentration. The mind wanders the twists and turns of the days, months, and years gone by. Thoughts of my first move came to mind. Actually it was my second, but I remember so little of the first one due to my young age.

It was the move out of the house I grew up in. Much like this move, I found myself with little time to think on what I was doing and plenty of excitement over what the change could mean. In the end it was less about what my choice but still a significant move. I can't ignore the fact that one part of my life ended the day the house I grew up in became just another mailbox on a street.

The rest area ahead promised vending machines and a scenic overlook. Apparently I was not quite done with those fries, or perhaps they were not done with me. I parked the car and shut off the engine. The heated July air fell upon me as the bubble of air conditioned bliss in my car popped when the door swung open.

The running joke in Arizona is that at least it's a dry heat. This much heat is never comfortable. Since this was to be our new normal, it was better to experience it at its worst. The signs warned of poisonous animals and not to leave the sidewalk. I decided to take a picture of the sign for an interesting Facebook post.

The view was alien to me. Sand but not beach, rocks but not shore, this East Coast native needed to find a way to acclimate to the color brown. Yet there was still some green. Beside me was a young girl in green shorts, walking a dog. Looked like some lab-beagle mix with a bit of German shepherd thrown in. The picnic tables were all re-painted green. The bark of the trees was green. Still, to my eyes the desert was not quite the new normal.

Leaving the rest stop behind, the promise of arriving at our new home was forcing my foot closer to the floor. The yearning of the heart for the home we left behind faded with each mile marker that passed. My ears popped as the car took the long road down from the mountains. Snaking this way and then that, I felt thankful that friction coupled with power brakes kept the edges of the road away from me. The emptiness of the desert filled the void at the edge of the road where the pavement cracked and fell away. Cacti came into view. Long, tall, green sentries with a halo of prickly flesh, they spoke to each other of seasons past. Seasons that only change on the calendar. They remembered a time when the mountain, and not the highway, rolled by.

The fifty miles to Phoenix had become twenty. ❧

Thorns

Vincent A. Alascia

The middle of March came up and caught me somewhere between the lion and the lamb. The ground, though newly defrosted, lacked the hint of green I longed to see. Though the air no longer held the chill of winter's shadow, it was not warm enough to be comfortable. I hoped for some sun, but the clouds kept the rays from my eyes. We had rain last night, and there would probably be more tonight. I could feel the weight of the moisture in the air.

I went out into the yard that afternoon just as my father used to. He always insisted on beginning the spring cleanup of the yard early. "This is the time to do it," he had often said. "Do it before the April rains come."

The task for today was to rid a small lilac bush of the vines that threatened to choke it. The thorny tendrils spread up from the very pit of Perdition. They wrapped, wound, and wrung the life from the small bush that my father had planted three years ago. Now was the best time for this job. There were neither leaves nor bees to hinder my task. I let it go too long last year and had to spend the summer worrying about losing the bush and scratching my arms on the thorns every time I mowed around it. Also I needed to be outside. I needed to breathe the air and feel the freedom that winter took from me.

My father hated being cooped up in the house. Maybe that's where I get it from. However, he would have taken care of the thorns last spring instead of putting the job off for another day. We cannot all be like our fathers, I guess.

Still, I felt like him as I walked to the shed. I retrieved a metal rake and an old lopping shear. I also had with me the new pruning shears I bought last week, the ones with the yellow handles. My dad had a knack for picking out the right tool for the job. I tried to get close.

I looked at the helpless lilac bush. Although a shrub, lilac can grow to be twenty feet high but you have to keep on them, pruning away the unwanted limbs. I tried the first year—or, I should say, my dad reminded me to keep at it the year before his death. The bush now stood ten feet or so, maybe taller if not for the thorns. It was not the largest one in the yard nor the smallest either. The thorny vines worked their way up to the highest limbs and pulled down the branches. They hung down, eager to snatch any passerby. The tree hardly flowered last spring, and this year I feared there would be no flowers at all.

My wife suggested cutting everything down—the thorns, the lilac, everything. I couldn't do that. "There's hope yet for that little tree," I said to her.

Besides, Dad would not have given up so easily. He knew more about trees, shrubs, and grass than he had time to teach me. Unfortunately, I had to take care of this one on my own.

I recalled the time I ran over the small cherry blossom tree he had just planted for my mother. I had only received my driver's license a week earlier, and this was the first time he let me take out the car. When I pulled the old Buick into the driveway, I cut the wheel too much to miss the lawn mower on the other side and nailed the tree. I don't know what magic he used or what trick he employed, but that tree lived and still stands today.

As I looked on the mess of vine and branch that stood before me, I realized the little pruning shears wouldn't do too much. I picked up the lopping shear. I snipped off a few thorny vines at the top and pulled them free from the lilac's branches with the rake. The thorns protested only mildly.

"See, this isn't so hopeless," I said to myself.

I freed a few more limbs from the clutches of the creeping vines, but I had to be careful. My gloves were not as thick as this job required, and the thorns were more than eager to snag my flesh. Little by little I trimmed away the vines. I grew bolder, searching out the thicker vines, hoping to release more of the tree. Pulling on the vine with my rake, the tree bent over but did not come free.

The limb I worked on snapped. My rake, now helplessly tangled in a mess of vine and branch, threatened to take down the whole tree. I stopped pulling. By twisting the rake and with only a little damage to the lilac, I freed it.

There must be another way, I thought. The branches hung low but did not touch the ground. If careful enough, I might be able to work my way up the lilac from the bottom. I squatted and crawled under the lower branches, taking care not to snag the collar of my flannel shirt on the thorns.

The vines ran down the thickest branches to the ground. Using the pruning shears as a spade, I cleared away the blanket of dead leaves until I could see where the thorns pushed through the ground. They slithered from their bed of earth and worms and continued up each branch. They twisted and wrapped around the lilac like a serpent.

"You have to watch out for the vines. They always find a way," Dad used to say. "They can twist and turn and come up anywhere."

Dad was certainly right on the mark with that. Many things in life find a way to creep up and get you. Dad taught me that too. I immediately thought of his sickness.

There was a lot to say about what cancer can do to a body. Fortunately Dad did not have the time to make too long a list. None of us did. I snipped away the thorns right at the ground as I thought about the past year. We no sooner learned of his condition, and it seemed as if we lost him. The cancer just came up and strangled the life out of him.

The irony is the very same man who told me to watch out for the vines could not do it himself. "Hopeless," he had said to me in the hospital. "Hopeless," my wife said this morning about the lilac.

I'll show them both hopeless. I began working on the thorns. Cutting every few inches, I twisted them off the branches.

I could not blame my father for getting sick, but I cannot forgive him for giving up so easily. "Lots of people beat this thing," I remember saying to him. He was not listening. He let it creep up on him and strangle him. He didn't put up the least bit of a fight.

Maybe Dad knew what he was up against. "You have to choose your fights," he once said. Maybe this was one fight he was not going to win, and he knew it. This lilac tree could go on resisting the creeping thorns until the very end, but its end would come. Despite all the resisting the thorns would kill it. That's just the way nature works.

"Then again, who says you can't fight nature?" I said to myself. I removed the thorny vines from the ground to above my head. Mind you, I was only kneeling beneath the lilac. I looked up. A maze of thorns and branches spread out above me. It became harder and harder to tell one from the other. I wiggled my arms and torso up between the branches I had cleared. I continued snipping along.

After a while I came to a point where I could stand. I had to slide my body up through the branches. It was tight, and if I had not already cleared these branches I would be missing a few layers of skin. All the cut pieces of thorns lying around my feet made me feel a little proud. Slowly I made progress. *Come supper time, there will not be a single thorn left in this lilac.* Then I noticed something to the right, just above my shoulder.

I looked closer. I had never noticed this from outside the lilac. A small nest sat tucked away in between the branches and where the thorns were the thickest. The nest consisted of pieces of twigs and straw tucked into a ball a little larger than a grapefruit. You would never have noticed it from the outside. The thorns enveloped the small nest.

Using the tip of my pruning shear, I carefully pushed aside some of the straw. Four bluish-gray eggs sat in a tightly packed circle. Above me I heard the manic chirping of a mother who, unknown to me, was always in view of her nest and little ones. I pulled the shear away and dropped it to the ground.

I looked at the nest and at the thorns around it, providing protection as only thorns can. I knew I couldn't go any further.

The thorns, wrapped tightly around the nest, dared me to disturb them. In one push or pull they could destroy that small nest. I knew it, and so did the thorns. The tiny birds inside probably did not. *Hostages, tiny sleeping hostages, not yet brought into this world,* I thought.

I wiggled out from beneath the lilac and inspected the shrub. I hoped to find another way. I knew removing the thorns without hurting the tree was possible, though I doubted that I could do so without tearing the nest apart. "The thorns had won," I said to myself. I raked out all that I had cleared away and hoped the remainder would wither and dry. Maybe I could try again in a month or so when the birds abandoned their nest.

"You have to know what you're fighting against, son." I remembered my Dad's words as I put the tools away. I guess sometimes it takes as much courage to know when not to fight.

As I walked into the house, I looked once more at the lilac. Maybe its chances were slim but not as slim as the chances of those eggs secure in their fortress of twigs and thorns. In that nest lay tiny hint of life and rebirth. There remained some hope hidden precariously among a thorny sarcophagus.

The late mid-day sun tried to poke through and ended up painting the clouds a crimson gray. The air was definitely a lot colder also. As I went in the house I could not help thinking that the thorns had won. ༄

Finally Getting to Say Goodbye

Helene Benigno-Stich

My sister, Christine, and I (aged five and seven, respectively) couldn't believe we had our very own dog. We'd been out running errands and saw-begged-and-received an adorable beagle/lab mix puppy from a guy just giving them away outside the mall. Sandy, as we called her, was wild and beautiful and smarter than she—or—we could handle.

During a lazy summer morning many months after we got Sandy, our dad was resting on a lounge chair in the backyard when a meter reader opened the gate and strode in unannounced. Sandy hid behind Dad's chair and then snuck over to the gate, cutting off the man's only retreat. Then she advanced and launched herself at the man's throat. Our dad had to use every ounce of strength to pull her off. I'm guessing the meter reader probably announced himself after that.

After a few other instances of Sandy playing a little too rough with the neighborhood kids (nobody got hurt but there were some close calls), our parents decided that the dog was a danger to others and took her away without any discussion with my sister or me.

"Sandy went to live with a nice lady on a farm," our mother explained. She still maintains that's exactly what happened, cliché though it is.

A couple of years later, just before Christmas, Tinsel found us. Some living heart donor had dumped the kitten in a neighborhood garbage in the cold. My sister and I saved her from the can and anxiously watched as she followed us home. Perhaps there was a little coaxing on our part. We felt a thrill of excitement as we opened the front door and she confidently stepped through. Running late to pick up our father from the train station, our mother hurried us right back out while scooting the little ball of fur onto our front porch. Christine and I prayed the cat would still be there when we returned, wisely using the time we had our parents captive in the car to wear them down.

Once home, we saw the little black-and-white kitten still hanging around. From there it was just one small step to get her back inside. The kitten shrewdly sealed the deal herself when she played adorably with the silver tinsel under our Christmas tree (hence the name Tinsel,) and with that Pet Number Two entered our lives.

Tinsel was beautiful and entertaining. We'd sing "How much is that doggie in the window?" and she would emit a long low meow in response to each chorus. I just knew she'd be a hit on David Letterman's "Stupid Pet Tricks" and tried in vain to talk my parents into contacting the show.

She was a great cat—until we moved. Who would have guessed that a new home just 20 minutes east would undo the Persian mix? From then on it was "Meow meow meow" to go out, and then she'd turn right around and "Meow meow meow" to come back in. My sister and I headed off to college soon after we moved, and our parents' sanity went first.

Finally, just before we returned for Christmas break, they took Tinsel to a shelter, doing the most dignified job they could of playing "ring and run." Once again, we didn't get a say nor did we get an opportunity to say goodbye to our cat of 10 years.

In my last year of college I surprised my mother with a puppy for her birthday. I'd had two choices: a full-breed bichon fries or a mixed yorkie/poodle. I chose the mixed breed (more acceptable for my college-age bank account.) Imagine my surprise when we found out the little guy was the bichon. In her defense, the breeder really *was* mostly blind.

Well, Jiggsie, as he came to be called, was the most adorable little puppy on the planet, and that was definitely for a reason. He was full-on crazy. A manic barker like no other, he started out "the best guard dog ever," then turned into a "grumpy old man" or just plain annoying, depending on who you asked.

He once chewed and clawed his way through a full-sized hotel door, simply because he didn't like being behind it. (Super fun explaining *that* to the front desk staff.) Jiggsie also ripped apart the garbage more times than my parents could count. Still, he was the apple of my father's eye.

Jiggsie's kidneys caused that final trip to the vet at age 15. My sister and I were married by this time. I was in Phoenix, Christine in Charlotte, and our parents lived in Tucson, so, again, there was no goodbye.

About a year before Jiggsie passed, I finally got my very own pile of fur. She was lost and alone in an Avondale Walmart parking lot, again just before Christmas. My fiancée, Perry, and I scooped up a little puppy that was in imminent danger of being killed by the frantic cars of holiday shoppers. Although in a hurry ourselves we spent quite a bit of time trying to find her owner but to no avail. She just sat in my arms, content as could be, this reddish-brown adorable ball of fur with the kindest, most beautiful eyes I'd ever seen. They were rimmed in black, and she melted my heart.

It was bad timing. We'd just moved into our newly built home two weeks earlier and were headed out of town for Christmas in just a few days. We called the local shelters and hung "lost dog" flyers all over the neighborhood, but we got no response. In the end, we deduced that an elderly woman had probably dumped her from a car. For the longest time the puppy was deathly afraid of two things: cars and women with white hair.

Tentatively moving forward, we took the puppy to the local animal hospital to get her checked out. She was proclaimed most likely a three-month-old and in perfect health. With a black tongue and lion-like mane, the vet guessed her to be a chow/golden retriever mix. Everyone in the office fawned over her chow looks and retriever demeanor. We admitted that it wasn't the best time for us to get a dog, and the vet offered to take her.

Needless to say, we named her Willow.

Willow only did two mischievous things in her first months with us, but, boy, were they whoppers. First, she chewed an actual hole in our brand new carpet, smack dab in the entranceway to our home where nobody could miss it. The second was worse. Arizonans know how difficult it can be to keep a perfectly manicured yard of grass in the best of circumstances. Well, Willow must have felt that landscaping wasn't enough of a challenge. One day I came home from a long day at work to find our newly laid backyard grass ripped up in its entirety. We yelled and cried at the cost and the mess and debated if we could afford to keep her, but she stared at us with those eyes of hers and we were undone.

As if sensing our disappointment in her, one of her pointed ears flopped soon after this episode, never to point again; with it went her mischievousness. I wish I had a dime for every time someone told us she was the best dog they'd ever met. There was not one chewed shoe, stolen piece of food, or torn-through trash. She didn't even bark unless she deemed it a major security breach.

She was the perfect dog, though perhaps not the brightest. Once while looking through our bedroom window, as some birds devoured my husband's newly laid grass seed, Perry teased her. "Look, Willow, look, it's birds, birds! Go get them!" Willow immediately launched herself from our bed into the air and head on into our window. Classic Willow, always trying to please us even at her own expense.

After I gave birth to my angelic daughter, Vivian, I started working full time from home, and Willow deemed it her job to stay by my side. From room to room she followed me, ever patient outside the door of the bathroom, bedroom, or wherever I was, planting herself right in my path.

Eventually both my daughter and I found out we were slightly allergic to Willow. We debated giving her away, and there was a list of offers within a day. A couple of people pled their cases of why they were more deserving than the others. In the end, we shaved down her gorgeous, long, auburn coat and kept her out of the bedrooms and went on with our lives. How could we ever part with Willow?

I'd love to say we never took her for granted, that we lavished all our free time on rubbing her belly and taking her for long walks, but our lives were a whirlwind of work and child rearing so we did what we could. At seven years old Vivian loved Willow so much, but after the toddler days Willow was now habitually tentative around her. My guess: too many tight, loving squeezes around the neck.

I can't tell you when I knew, but I knew. One day it took a fraction longer for her to get up, but we just said she was getting older. It was now nine-and-a-half years since we found her in that Walmart parking lot. A couple of weeks later she coughed up one dime-sized spot of blood. I suggested taking her to the vet but Perry came up with a half-dozen things it could be, so we just watched her closely.

Then one day we woke to find Vivian screaming for us. It looked like a scene from a horror movie. Blood was everywhere, so alarming an amount that we wondered how Willow was still conscious. We immediately brought her to our vet. A couple of days later the vet called with the worst news: advanced cancer, all over her lungs. They hadn't been able to pinpoint the origin, just where it had spread to. Her cough increased, and her breathing became heavily labored with any kind of movement.

"Keep her comfortable," said the vet from the same animal hospital where we took her nine years earlier, "then give me a call when it's time."

Vivian was eagerly planning a party for Willow's 10th birthday, which was only a little more than a month away, but I knew making it to that birthday was a long shot. Still, in some ways she hadn't changed at all. Willow continued to stare at me with those eyeliner-rimmed, soft, kind eyes and tried her best to follow me around and lie by my side, until the final couple of days when she only moved when she had to.

Finally, on August 4th, she let us know. It was a typically brutal summer day in Arizona, but Willow still drank copious amounts of water. Despite that she could not go to the bathroom. It took supreme effort for her just to breathe as she stood and followed us outside to try to pee, exerting more will to please than actual physical strength.

My husband and I dropped Vivian with a friend and drove to the vet with Willow for the last time. She walked in by herself, and I wondered for the hundredth time if we were doing the right thing. If she could walk, difficult as it was, wasn't there still some quality of life left?

The vet examined her and declared that this was it.

My husband and I held on to her. There was no way I was going to let her die alone with a stranger. She stared at me as the first shot was administered; Perry and I told her over and over how much we loved her and thanked her for being in our lives. Then she gently closed her eyes. She didn't move for the second shot. I couldn't believe how fast she was gone. I felt like my heart would explode.

I had complained my whole life that I'd never gotten a chance to say goodbye to a pet. Well, as they say, be careful what you wish for. The hole Willow's absence left felt horrible, and our house stayed in perpetual mourning. Our daughter begged daily for another dog. An only child, she was going through the death of her best friend at the tender age of seven. How could we refuse her?

This time I did my research. I knew we had supremely lucked out with Willow but she was also taken from us so early, and who wanted to go through that again? After weeks of research on breeds, we found a short list of those with hearty life spans who were also minimum shedders. We ended up with Snickers, an American cocker spaniel who was born on the 4th of July. As I write this she's about to turn two. She was from a line of champion show dog parents with a long, healthy lineage.

We love her to pieces, and she is one of the smartest, cutest, and most talented dogs we've ever met. She closes the drawer after I fetch her leash from it, plays soccer better than we can, jumps through hoops, rolls over, dances in circles on her two hind legs, and a half-dozen other tricks that we barely had to even teach her. She also chews up every available pen, sock, and tissue she can find and will bark at anyone new. She's also a champion snuggler, and her favorite thing to do is curl up in your lap and sleep away the afternoon.

The hole Willow left does not go away. Attention shifts, time is taken up, and our minds wander to her less. But I know we were given a gift with our first dog, both by her presence and in finally getting to say goodbye. ∾

Grandfather and the Saguaro

Jen Bielack

I remember well the last time my grandfather told the story of the saguaro. He was sitting in his favorite chair, his aching feet propped on a pillow on the coffee table, nothing important on TV. I sat curled in the corner of the nearest couch.

"So, *abuelito*, why don't you tell me that story about the saguaro?"

"The *saguarito, hita*," he said back to me. He liked using the short form—which in Spanish was really the longer form—for most words. Thus I was "Carmelita" and my brother "Juanito."

"Well," said he, "the saguaros are reminders to all of us—*gabachos, mexicanos, indios, chinos, negros* . . ."

Sometimes now he would forget to finish a sentence.

"Reminders of what?" I prompted.

"Reminders of where we are and where we come from, us *mexicanos*. These green giants stretch all the way from Guaymas in Sonora to Phoenix and beyond to the north. They speak silently, but if you have Mexican blood you will hear what they say: 'This land where I stand, *esta tierra*, this is Mexico.'"

"But, *abuelito*, we live in Arizona, not in Mexico." I knew this would bring forth a feisty response.

"But it used to be Mexico, Carmelita. It was stolen. All this land was taken from Mexico not that long ago. Only the saguaros mark the territory. They are the guardians of the land."

"Tell me more, *mi abuelo*. Tell me more about your saguaro."

His face crinkled, and he smiled with his mouth and his eyes.

"Yes, I met a saguaro one night in the desert. He saved my life."

"Tell me the story."

"Well," he began, then interrupted himself. "First fix my pillow, would you?"

To do this I had to support both legs just above his ankles with one arm while I flipped the pillow with the other. Then I gently let his heels back down onto the fresh side of the pillow. His feet were very sensitive.

"Gracias, Carmelita. So this was many years ago when my skin was smooth like the palo verde, *pero* not green *por su puesto*."

"Of course," I encouraged him.

"We were crossing the Sonoran Desert, not far from the town they call Sierra Vista. We walked at night under the light of the moon. They had no fancy cameras then, no balloons floating in the sky."

I knew that Grandfather referred to the blimp that scanned the desert near the Sierra Vista for border crossers.

"It was my first crossing, but for *mi primo* it was the second *y para mi tio*, he lost count by then. We slept in the shade of a deep *arroyo durante el dia. Por la noche*, we walked. And those saguaros, they walked with us, but if you looked at them they were never moving. They only moved when you weren't looking."

I stifled a giggle, and he gave me a look.

"*Es verdad, hita.* They walked. They're still out there, walking."

"Then what happened?"

"Then I got ahead of the others. Like you, I thought I was so smart back then. *Muy inteligente*."

Now I gave him a look, but he ignored me.

"So one minute I'm walking straight ahead, *todo derecho*, following a path as plain as day, and the next minute, smack, I walk right into a saguaro."

"What did you do?"

"I did what anybody would do. I screamed like a baby. That saguaro stuck me in so many places: *la cabeza, las manos*, even my knees got stuck with those little needles that look like hairs.

"So after that we stopped for the night. We camped right there. *Mi tio* made a gigantic fire. He put me so close to that fire I thought I would melt. Then he took his pliers from his *mochila*, and he pulled out those needles one by one, all that he could."

"Did you cry, *abuelito*?"

"No, I didn't cry. I was prepared for that pain."

"But why do you always call that saguaro 'your' saguaro, *abuelito*?"

"Because in the morning when we could see better, we looked at that saguaro. It was in the same place, right in the middle of the path. It was not there when I was walking the night before. It stepped in front of me at the last minute."

"What last minute?"

"The last minute before I was going to fall to my death. That last minute."

Now Grandpa paused so that he could tell the next part very slowly and carefully.

"Carmelita, behind that saguaro, mi saguaro, the ground dropped for one hundred feet. One—hundred—feet—of nothing but air. *Mi saguarito*, he saved my life, *mi hita*."

"Wow," I said, like I was hearing it for the first time. I still got shivers sometimes when he reached the end of his story.

"Look," said Grandpa, "look here. Feel here." He pointed to the hard part of his forehead up towards his hairline.

I leaned forward and stretched my hand toward his head. He guided my fingertips to a sort of callus under his skin.

"Feel that, Carmelita?"

I nodded solemnly.

"That's where *mi saguarito* kissed me. That part of me is saguaro. Those needles went in and never came out."

I continued to rub his forehead gently with my fingertips because I knew he liked it. He closed his eyes and smiled just with his mouth.

"Be careful," he whispered. "You don't want to get those needles in you."

"I think they're too deep, *abuelito*." I sat back down all the way and waited quietly. Sometimes he had other words of wisdom to impart, though I was pretty sure I had heard them all by now.

"You know, I think that's where I went wrong, Carmelita," he suddenly volunteered.

21

"What do you mean, where you went wrong?" I scrunched up my face.

"Well, I stopped walking, you see. I wasn't a good *saguarito*. When my feet got bad, I stopped walking. Now," he said, indicating his feet in their faded slippers on the pillow, "these things are almost useless to me." He shook his head. "It's a bad way to end when you're part cactus."

"It's okay, *abuelito*." I patted his arm. "You're going to be okay."

But he wasn't. Within a month he took to his bed. Within another the ambulance was at our door, taking him to a hospital room where he lay like a skeleton, his head turned toward the window, though there was nothing much to see. One night while he was asleep, I taped a magazine picture of a big old saguaro on the window where he could see it if he opened his eyes.

I was in school the day he died. My mother told me he did open his eyes and did see the saguaro and that he smiled. I like to think he saw it at the last minute.

At his funeral a few days later, choked with sadness, I retold his saguaro story to the small throng of family and friends who came to bid him farewell.

Afterwards, I had a chance to speak to the son of the cousin Grandfather crossed the desert with that time.

"You know, my father always talked about that saguaro too," my uncle* told me in a soft voice. "He remembered it his whole life."

"Yes, it was quite the miracle, wasn't it?" I forced a sad smile.

"Have you ever been to the Sonoran Desert south of Sierra Vista?"

"No, never. Why? Have you? Did you find that saguaro?" I was suddenly very motivated, already planning my own future pilgrimage to the spot.

"Well, that's just it. I've been there, and I don't know if you know about saguaros. They don't grow much above 4,000 feet in elevation. The area around Sierra Vista and south into Mexico is much higher than that. In that part of the desert, there aren't any to be seen."

We both stood in silence for a while. I thought of the small knot on Grandpa's forehead, his swollen and useless feet. His life. His death. His *saguarito*. Then I smiled.

"Well," I said to my uncle, "that saguaro must have walked an awfully long ways." ✍

Glossary

abuelo/abuelito—grandfather, grandpa
-ita, -ito—suffix meaning "little" (term of endearment)
hita—little girl/daughter
gringos/gabachos—slang terms for "whites" or non-Mexicans
indios—Indians
chinos—Chinese
negros—African Americans
mi—my
esta tierra—this land
palo verde—desert tree with smooth green bark
pero—but
por su puesto—of course
primo—cousin
tio—uncle
durante el dia—during the day
por la noche—at night
es verdad—it's true
muy inteligente—very smart
todo derecho—straight ahead
la cabeza—the head
las manos—the hands
mochila—backpack

*older cousin may be called "uncle" in Chicano families

Oak Creek Rising

Jen Bielack

Oak Creek, Sedona, Arizona, January 27, 2013

I live in a beautiful place; let me just say that right up front. The elevation and latitude of this northern Arizona spot have conspired to bestow elements of other beautiful places upon her, coupled with her own stark red rock panoramas that bring people trekking from Asia and Australia and all points in between. I say "her" because Sedona is feminine in so many ways, starting with her namesake, Sedona Schnebly, a frontier woman from Missouri who homesteaded here.

You can actually glimpse a red leaf or two in the fall, not just yellow like most Southwestern woods. Blackberries and mint grow wild in abundance as they do in New England. And water is everywhere, some days more than others.

I live part time, along with my cat, in a small mobile home park a few miles up Oak Creek Canyon on the back road to Flagstaff. My mobile home is almost as old as me: I'll be sixty-three this summer and it'll be fifty-five. It's eight feet wide, like they made them back then. But who needs indoor space when my backyard runs up and down different canyons and side creeks, and my front yard is Oak Creek itself?

It's been raining off and on here—mostly on—for about forty-eight hours and is expected to keep raining intermittently for another twenty-four hours. That translates to between three and four inches of rain. I was headed into town yesterday to run some extracurricular errands but hadn't even left my driveway before I ran into a stranded fisherman, dressed to the nines in creek-fishing gear. I mean, he had the waterproof bib-overalls that transition into boots at the bottom. He sported a camouflage multi-pocketed vest, a hat graced with fishing flies.

"Is there a bridge back across to the other side?" he asked me more than conversationally.

"Yeah, there's one right around the corner. Why?"

"I was fishing down the creek a ways and got stuck on this side when all this water came rushing down. It was like a dam burst."

I wasn't sure how he even crossed the creek but I directed him to the bridge, barely above water itself, where he found his fishing buddy parked on the other side.

I also tried to explain to him that he had been lucky to escape what was more likely a "flash flood." I gave him the short version. This is the longer one.

Oak Creek is a canyon that lies at around 4200 feet in elevation where I live. That elevation climbs steadily towards Flagstaff but probably doesn't change more than five hundred feet. It is surrounded by mountains, high and low. Even close to Sedona there are some six thousand footers that get snow when it's raining down below. The closer to Flagstaff, the higher the mountains above the creek and the more snow on them in wintertime.

Until this past week it had been cold for about a month, below freezing at night in Sedona and not much higher than that in the daytime in Flagstaff thirty miles away. Both my son and I, at different times, have hiked up to the nearby snow level in recent weeks and saw very little run-off. One of our favorite side canyons, Casner, was frozen over where water had pooled from a previous run-off. My son follows some side trails not marked for hikers that he calls "waterfall trails," because that's just what happens when the snow melts or a heavy rain comes. He had been disappointed with the freezing conditions up until now.

Needless to say, he won't be disappointed if he gets up here anytime soon. It has stayed above freezing for the last week, and the weekend rain just added a bolstering nudge to that frozen snow up high. The bridge that I normally take to come and go has temporarily disappeared beneath a raging creek. Thankfully there's a much higher bridge about a mile farther up that I can cross.

After directing the fisherman to the bridge (now under water), I decided not to go to town after all. Instead I hung around the bridge in the pouring rain and took photos of three kayakers who had portaged around the bridge and were getting ready to put in again. I had never seen kayaks like theirs, short and snub-nosed. And these guys were dressed to do battle, with helmets and padding everywhere and some kind of compact flotation device on their chests.

Where they were going to enter the water, on the south side of the bridge, the landscape had changed drastically. A myriad of different-sized rocks and boulders normally stand well above the water line, and a kayaker wouldn't dream of boating there. The creek had swelled to twice its size with almost no rocks in sight now.

I looked north to where two massive dead trees had been trapped for months when the waters receded from a previous flood. There yesterday, they were nowhere to be seen today, which means they easily cleared the bridge.

I went back indoors to get out of the pelting rain and bided my time until noon to venture forth again, wearing my own funky rain gear: a pair of calf-high red rubber boots with good tread (that did not leak) and a camouflage rain poncho to keep my legs dry, along with a hat, hood, etc. I really lucked out, because it only rained a little at the beginning and end of my hour-and-a-half trek. In fact, I was too hot most of the time. Impermeable materials do that to you.

My goal was to visit my favorite spots on the creek and see how they looked after the transformation by the flood. I have these two places where I go to swim in the summertime. One is near what my son calls "the jacuzzi," a slight turn in the creek punctuated by a tumble of good-sized rocks, not huge or car-sized, but big enough to sit on or lean against where the water "boils." Just below that boiling water is where I would slip in and follow a pathway between underwater rocks down to an open spot where I reached a large flat-topped rock, just below the surface, turned, and swam back. Swimming with the current going down and against it coming back. An idyllic spot to swim, fish lurking below me.

Today I got within fifteen feet of the spot, but our usual path to it—where we duck under a fallen log (that I once smacked my head on)—was under water. And near the jacuzzi the water had roiled into white bubbles. I saw this bubble effect several times but only near the edges of the creek where the water got trapped in eddies.

There's another great place to swim where many folks go, especially on weekends, that I simply call "the beach." There used to be a rope swing there, but the tree it hung from sort of self (or people) destructed. This place can be magical on an early summer morning during the week when it's deserted. The fairly low sun hits a wide, deep spot in the creek, and the reflection from the water dances on an east-facing red canyon wall. It is mesmerizing, this play of dancing light, making this a great meditation spot.

It's also a spot for dogs. My own dog, Bolo, adverse to our swimming pool in Tempe, would walk right into Oak Creek until the water was chest deep and started swimming. He would play at the beach with a leggy Irish setter, named Boulder, who lives nearby. That was in July of 2010. In December we placed poor Bolo's ashes in the water there. He made it to fourteen.

But I still see Boulder all the time on my hikes, he and his sister, Puma, a smaller black dog quite similar in stature to Bolo. They play this game where Puma "chases" Boulder into the water and won't let him back out. Boulder, who can get in the creek year-round, will stay in the water up to his belly until Puma gets distracted, and then he makes a run for it. I've distracted Puma several times myself because I just couldn't bear seeing Boulder in that freezing water so long.

Couldn't get near the beach today. The path that winds down to it among blackberry bushes (and even a tad of poison ivy and, trust me, I know poison ivy when I see it) was flooded where it normally crosses a nearly dry side creek. So odd to see a well-worn path with water coming up it. Then the ground rises up a little ways, and you follow a partly sandy, partly rocky path flanked by giant sycamores through small trees to the beach.

All that looked to be underwater today from where I was forced to stop. I have a small inkling now of what floods do to familiar landscapes; they obliterate them.

My last stop was Casner Canyon. This was the spot where my son and I had hiked a couple weeks ago to find thick ice. We didn't test our weight on it; the water underneath was ice-cold and several feet deep. But it easily held the biggest rock we could throw onto it. This is an infrequently running creek that you can cross and take a path up the other side that leads you along run-off areas (waterfalls) and up to some nice views west and north. As I headed down towards the smaller canyon, I stopped at a spot where I could clearly hear the water from Oak Creek and the run-off in Casner Creek. They say you can't attend to two sounds at the same time and it's true, but I listened to them alternately. The more I descended towards Casner the more dominating was its sound, and I could see it running from a stopping place only halfway down, a rare thing indeed.

No disappointment. Casner Creek was running full-throttle, the water alternately a coffee-with-cream color and white foam. The pool that had been ice-bound not long ago had a huge pile of frothy bubbles in one corner. There would be no crossing it, not today. I took a photo where we normally crossed: a large black tree with a massive trunk is on the far side. A series of stepping stones that normally takes you across, nowhere to be seen today.

When the rain lets up and the weather turns cold again, as it may do over the next few days, I expect the creek waters will subside. I know I'll be swimming in my favorite spots by June, maybe sooner, in the new wetsuit I bought. It is beautiful here, even in these times of high water and flooding. I know that's not the case everywhere, so I feel particularly grateful to be able to take shelter in my cozy 1958 mobile home with no fear of being washed away. And if you haven't, you may want to visit "Red Rock Country"—Sedona—and Oak Creek one of these days. ✑

Betrayal and Hope in the Desert

Carmela Ayello Bottita

Jeff and I chose Arizona to live out our retirement dreams. A large settlement I had received helped set our financial situation in order. We purchased a townhouse in Scottsdale, investing conservatively in mutual funds. After a year the stairs were too much for me, so we gave the townhouse to the kids and moved to Goodyear. They followed us a year later, moving eight blocks from us, close enough to help out when we asked and far enough for us to stay out of each other's business.

The one thing I missed from our original home in Pennsylvania was my medical team and support group. Several years earlier I had received a diagnosis of Eosinophilia-myalgia syndrome (EMS,) a condition caused in part by a contaminated batch of tryptophan produced in Japan. The tryptophan was one of the components in L-tryptophan, a health food supplement sold as a sleep aid.

EMS shows up with a considerable number of symptoms that often look like other diseases. My medical team in Pennsylvania had experience with the syndrome, but my doctor in Arizona had never dealt with it. The symptoms vary in intensity and frequency, making it difficult to treat—something Jeff never really understood.

Jeff thought that after we settled with the company in Japan, my symptoms would magically disappear. He ignored it when the doctor said my health would never return to normal, and through the years I developed other conditions related to the damage done to my immune system. Jeff just wrote me off as a hypochondriac, and his attitude slowly drove a permanent wedge between us.

Even with my medical difficulties, one positive thing about

moving was the weather. The warmer weather helped ease the constant pain, and I became more active. Even in the summer when it was more than 100 degrees, I could swim every day. I began to make new friends once we moved to Goodyear and settled into a new lifestyle.

My dear friend from Pennsylvania moved to Tucson. I started visiting her at least twice a year to get rejuvenated. In her home and the quiet of Green Valley, a Tucson suburb, I found the inner peace that had begun to slip away when I was in my own home. I hardly noticed it at first. It was if the heat of the desert consumed whatever inner harmony I once thought I had. A mysterious restlessness had begun to set in.

In Green Valley I found peace. Maybe it was the surroundings: the mountains, quiet streets. The air seemed fresher and the weather milder. I felt a tranquility come over me the minute I stepped into my friend's home. It was quiet—no TV blaring and people treating each other with kindness and respect. It occurred to me that I could not remember the last time Jeff talked to me with any respect; he preferred to humiliate me in front of people. I didn't have the courage to leave, and I didn't want to stay. So Tucson became my refuge.

Jeff began to withdraw a few thousand dollars from our funds to pay bills or travel. That's what I was led to believe, and I never had a reason to worry about finances. He handled them because he was better at it.

Jeff started going to the casino once a month. I never thought much of it. I had watched him play black jack for years. He never stayed at a table where the dealer was hot and always left when he was ahead. Of course he lost, but Jeff always kept it within whatever limit he had set.

In December we took the family on a New Year's cruise. Jeff would go to the casino at night while I would see the shows or go to the piano bar to listen to the music. The family made it a point to have dinner together every night.

When making a purchase on the ship, I found that our credit card was maxed out. There had to be a mistake, I thought.

The card had a $6000 limit, and I knew that when we left home there was less than a $1000 balance on it. So where did the other $5000 go? I told Jeff about the card; he said not to worry. An hour later Jeff found me and told me there had been an error and the account was fixed. I had no reason not to believe him.

In January I checked our bank account. I hadn't done it in several months, so I looked all the way back to June. I saw hundreds of dollars in ATM withdrawals from the same casino in Arizona, as much as $1000 in one day. Then I checked our credit card and saw that there were cash advances that totaled close to $5000 aboard the cruise ship casino. The advances were paid with a credit card I didn't know about.

I asked where the large deposits had come from. Jeff said he was having a good run at the casino. The deposits and the withdrawal dates seemed to verify his story. Later I would discover he covered his losses with withdrawals from our mutual fund investment. When I questioned the casino advance on the ship, he said he had taken care of it.

Something wasn't right, and I was going to find out.

I called the cruise line and asked them to send me copies of each transaction. Sure enough, he had lost more than $5000 gambling. Every withdrawal had his signature on it. I checked the investment account and saw a six-thousand-dollar withdrawal made a few days after we returned from the cruise and a large payment made to the credit card to cover the charges.

When I confronted him, he got very nasty and told me he handled the money and to mind my own business. I can't remember ever yelling, let alone accusing him of stealing my money until that day. I got tired of asking for money when he always had a couple of thousand dollars in his account. My Social Security was being deposited into our common house account, and I began transferring half of my Social Security into my own checking account every month. I would soon realize it was too little too late.

We shared the same house, but we didn't share any trust and whatever love we might have had died years ago. We argued about everything now. I asked him if he took care of the reverse mortgage and if he had paid the balance of his life insurance loans. One day I said, "Jeff, is everything up to date? If something happens to you, I need to know things are taken care of, that I will have a roof over my head."

"That will be your problem, not mine."

His answered disturbed me. I should have pushed the issue, but I let it go.

Then Jeff's health began to slip. He began to lose weight. He ate less, and we struggled to get him to stay hydrated. He began to lose his balance and fall. Looking back I wonder how much of his illness was from guilt.

Finally I got him to the hospital. They found that one lung had filled with fluid and the other had a spot and that the lining was pulling away. After asking Jeff a few questions about where he worked and if he was in the service, he received a diagnosis of mesothelioma. He was losing ground quickly, and they moved him to Hospice of the Valley for five days then home. My daughter and I cared for him with the help of hospice staff until he died on June 22, 2012. Since he never gained enough strength for a biopsy, we were unable to put in an insurance claim for mesothelioma.

As my daughter and I prepared for Jeff's funeral, getting the paperwork together that one needs, I discovered the betrayal that left me with almost nothing. Jeff never put my name on the reverse mortgage when I turned 62. I had less than $40,000 left of my settlement, and there was only $7000 left of Jeff's $40,000 life insurance. Then a week later I found out that he had used all the equity in the house, and I would need $187,000 dollars to save my home even though it was only worth $100,000.

I was going to lose my home and I hadn't known it. How did I not know? Did he know all along? How do you deal with the fact that one morning you wake up and suddenly realize that everything you thought you knew was a lie? The secure future that I believed I would have was gone, unexpectedly stripped from me.

At Jeff's memorial service several widows told me that the loss would get easier. If they only knew that I felt no grief. No, I felt anger and betrayal so potent I barely could contain my rage. I wanted someone to feel the hurt as bad as I did but not from grief.

It would be a long stressful summer for both my daughter and me. My daughter faced her own challenges when she began divorce proceedings. Before her father died I told her not to worry, that they could move in with me. But now there was no house to move in to. Fortunately Anna got to stay in her home with the kids, and I moved in with them too.

That summer I also found out that two of my stories were chosen to be published, and I began working on edits. This process helped me regain my confidence. I began to realize that I had a talent to tell a story.

When Anna, the kids, and I finally moved into her home after we painted, redecorated, bought new furniture and appliances, we began to live a new life based on love and, most importantly, honesty. Both the kids were happier, and Anna was able to find her own self-worth.

In the year since Jeff died I have found that I am the master of my own destiny. I have new hope and a purpose that I never thought was possible. Anna and the kids say that I smile and laugh more, and it's true. The doctors have said that I'm doing better. My blood work is better, and I'm dealing with the daily pain more positively. My illness no longer controls my life, my life controls my illness.

Hope is only found when one deals with the joy killers who sabotage your life. One must first be willing to look deep into them and find who and what those joy killers are.

This verse has become my guiding light and hope for my future in the dessert.

Jeremiah 29:11: "For I know the plans I have for you," declares the Lord, "plans to prosper you and not to harm you, plans to give you hope and a future." ∾

It's a Dry Heat

Donna Bowring

In the mid-1960s and early 1970s we were a family chasing the American dream, upwardly mobile, and on the move whenever my husband, Owen, accepted a job with a larger paycheck. We packed up six kids and our belongings four times in nine years.

We moved up and down the East Coast three times, twice for better jobs and once when Owen lost his job as the result of a plant shutdown. We moved from upstate New York to south Florida with $900 cash in hand and fingers crossed. Our moving caravan included Owen and our oldest son, OB, in a U-Haul leading the way, and me and the other five kids following in a 1961 Cadillac with rear fins that could cut another car in half.

Once we reached Florida we took up residence in a cheap motel. Owen took the kids to look for an affordable rental, and I went job hunting. I immediately landed a night position as a typesetter for *The Palm Beach Post*. Owen found a two-bedroom rental house and two days later went to work as a truck driver. The living arrangement was frustrating for a married couple, but when you're broke you take what you can get.

After a year of living in a tiny rented house (a ton of fun with six kids, I might add,) we had saved enough to buy a bigger home and Owen eventually worked his way back into the semiconductor business.

I fervently hoped we'd stay put for years. I wanted to nest permanently. However, Owen was still on the lookout for a heftier paycheck. At least once a month recruiters visited Florida, and he inevitably went the dinner, drinks, and "we'll-get-back-to-you-in-a-couple-of-weeks" route. I knew in the back of my mind there was always the possibility of another move and braced myself for "Hey, honey, I got a great offer, guess where?"

As time passed the thought of moving drifted to the back of my mind. Palm Beach Gardens was our home. We lived there for more than five years. I found myself lulled into a false sense of permanence, assuming the kids would grow up in Florida. Owen and I would retire there, watch the sun set on swaying palms, and perhaps play a round of golf. I looked forward to the golden years.

"I've been offered a new job," Owen said as we sat enjoying a drink after dinner in a posh restaurant. I should have known something was up; my husband rarely suggested that we eat out.

"Where?" I asked with a sigh.

"Arizona."

"My God, it's hotter than hell out there!"

"They have air conditioning, and everyone says it's a dry heat."

"Hot is hot," I said, "and I'm not real keen on moving again."

"The salary is ten thousand more a year."

I knew then we would be packing up yet again.

Upon hearing of the impending move our three boys, OB (Owen III,) 15, Jeff, 14, and Derek, 13, immediately balked at the idea. They turned into sullen little snots. They skipped school with the mistaken idea that I wouldn't find out, which of course I did. I drove to their favorite fishing hideout, and they were so surprised to see me they forgot to run.

They dawdled in the mornings until I shoved them out the door so they'd be on time for school. They dribbled home in the afternoon from twenty minutes to a half-hour late. They put off homework and bedtime until I told them if they wanted to grow up ignorant and sleep deprived it was on them. I would still kick them out when they turned eighteen.

Our girls, DeeDee, 12, Nikki, 10, and Marnie, 9, vented their displeasure by turning into whiners and pouters. Picking up dirty clothes and cleaning their room produced deep sighs as if they were in a forced labor camp.

I knew leaving Florida would be hard for them and I understood, but that did not allow them to be a collective pain in the butt. They were the Bowring six-pack (as they were called,) and at that moment I was ready to disown them all.

Owen left for his new job in March, blithely packing his bag and heading off while I stayed behind to sell the house and to allow the kids to finish the school year in Florida. I felt strongly that changing schools at that point would only lead to further chaos.

A couple of bonuses did come with his job. His new employer was paying to move our household, and travel arrangements came gratis through a local agency.

On a Saturday morning shortly after Owen left, I corralled all six of my little darlings, sat them down at the dining room table, and gave them a lecture, complete with the "Mom look," which consisted of the frown, the pursed lips, the crossed arms, and the shaking of the head.

"I know you don't want to move, and I know you know you have to. Pile on your complaints right now. I don't want to hear you grousing from today until the day we move."

"Why can't we stay here, and Dad can send us money so we won't have to move?" asked Nikki.

"Because that's not the way family works."

"None of us wants to go," said Jeff.

"Since you are under eighteen, you still have to go with your mother and father. When you reach the age of reason, you can go where you want."

"We'll run away," he threatened.

"Make sure you pack enough for the rest of your life, because I'm not coming to look for you."

"But there's no beach," moaned OB, "there's no water. It's a desert!"

"Of course there's water in Phoenix," I said, remembering the map of Arizona I had purchased as a way to familiarize myself with the state. "There are lakes and rivers and canals all around Phoenix."

"It won't be the same," Derek grumbled.

"Don't complain; you'll get used to it."

He slumped in his chair like a deflated balloon.

"I don't wanna leave my friends," Marnie announced.

"You'll make new ones. Won't that be fun?"

"No." She stomped her foot, and I grabbed her shirttail before she could leave the room in a hissy fit.

"Sit," I said. "We're not done."

"Mom," Nikki asked, "what state is Arizona in?"

"Arizona *is* a state, dummy," said OB.

"Mom! He called me a dummy."

"That's enough, OB. Do you know where Arizona is on the map?"

"Out west somewhere?"

"Close," I said. "There's an atlas in the bookcase. Go see what you can discover about your new home."

"Mom," DeeDee interrupted, "we are gonna take Frisky, aren't we?"

"Yes, of course, he's coming with us."

The girls had found a kitten near the baseball diamond when he was a tiny ball of fuzz and gave him his name. The inevitable "Can we keep him?" had followed after they found him. Why not, I thought. How much trouble could a cat cause?

After four years, I ate my words. He had grown into a monstrous, 17-pound tomcat with the disposition of a hungry tiger. He sat under a lemon tree in our front yard and attacked anything, human or animal, that dared trespass on his territory. He bit off the ear of a small dachshund that dug a hole under the fence from the neighbor's yard to ours.

Frisky did not meow, he hissed. His yellow eyes followed me around the house like a predator scoping out his dinner. I detested that cat, and I swore he knew how I felt.

The house sold in May, and the closing would take place in June. I had the logistics of moving down pat. The closing was on a Thursday. The last day of school was Friday, the day the movers would arrive. We would spend the weekend in a hotel and Monday morning embark on what I hoped would be an uneventful trip to our new home.

Our travel agent called me at the hotel to wish us luck and "Oh, by the way, your cat is too big for a cat carrier. You'll have to put him in a dog carrier and check him through with the luggage." The girls were sure he would die in the belly of the plane, and I assured them the damn cat was too mean to die. He would probably get out of his cage and chew up the entire luggage bay. The airline sent a carrier to the hotel. It took all three boys to load him in—two to hold his legs and one to shove him in and latch the door shut.

The morning we left for the airport, the boys wore matching flower-patterned pants. Not little girly-girl flowers, but big, splotchy psychedelic flowers. I reasoned they would be easier to keep track of if they stood out from everyone else. They were mortified—not because of the flowered pants, but because they had to dress alike. Nothing hurts the fragile young male ego so much as having to dress like your brothers. The girls were in matching dresses for the same identification reason but dared not say a thing after they saw how their brothers' complaints came to no avail.

As the ticket agent handed me our boarding passes, she informed me the airline did not deliver animals in cages to other terminals. I would have to pick up the cat after we got off the plane in Houston and carry it to the terminal where we would catch our flight to Phoenix. We only had an hour layover, and I hoped that it would be enough time to transport Frisky. Otherwise, I might dissolve in a puddle of tears.

"Goddamned cat tried to scratch me," said the baggage attendant in Houston.

"Calm down, Frisky," I said. The cat flipped his tail at me.

"Grab this carrier," I said to Jeff.

"Not me," he answered, "it's not my cat."

"I'm not going to argue whose cat it is. We have to go two terminals over to catch the plane to Phoenix, and you don't want to see me if we miss our flight."

He looked at me a second, must not have liked what he saw, and said, "Okay, okay, I'll take it."

I gathered the kids into a little group and ordered, "Follow me. Do not speak, do not turn right or left, and do not even contemplate stopping. And don't dawdle. Keep up with me."

I took off at a half-walk, half-run. I was on a mission. There was no way I was going to miss the flight to Phoenix. People turned to stare as though they had never seen a woman with six kids and a hissing, howling cat running through an airport terminal.

I guessed we were about halfway to our destination when I heard a beep-beep and an extended golf cart pulled up alongside me.

"Need a ride?" asked the man driving.

"I thought your cart was for handicapped passengers."

He looked at the kids, the cat in a dog cage, and me and said, "You qualify. Hop on."

We arrived at our terminal just as they announced boarding would begin in ten minutes. I checked the cat through luggage, got our boarding passes, and sent a prayer upstairs that the man in the cart would live a long and happy life.

Once on the plane I hustled the kids to the very back of the plane, close to the bathrooms. I fell into my seat, heaved a huge sigh of relief, and looked around to count heads, just to make sure I hadn't lost anyone.

Marnie was sure they would ride horses to school, past saloons and tumbleweeds blowing in the breeze, and there would be cowboys and Indians on every corner. Derek heard the pilot announce it was 110 degrees in Phoenix and decided he would probably die when he left the plane. Grumbling continued from the seats behind me until the flight attendants started showering the kids with cookies, peanuts, and sodas. In return Jeff rendered his dead-on John Denver impression and his passable Elvis hip swing and sneer, done to a slightly off-key version of "Jail House Rock."

As we disembarked the plane on steps rolled up to the main plane hatch, I thought, *I have arrived in hell.* Nikki tried running down the steps, landed on the tarmac, and skinned both knees. We walked through a tunnel barely cooler than outside and finally arrived inside the terminal. I was so glad to see Owen I almost cried. I don't know whether it was from relief that we finally made it or because I hadn't seen him for so long.

The house Owen bought was waiting to close until the owner signed the papers for the new house he was buying, which would be in two weeks. For that period, Owen's company paid for our stay in a motel. At least we had three adjoining rooms, and while not my idea of comfort at least it provided Owen and me some privacy.

"It's got a pool!" the kids chorused before our bags were unpacked. In the first few days they tentatively explored the area. Owen bought a leash for Frisky so DeeDee could take him out when nature called. Being around the pool daily, the kids made friends as kids always do. OB ogled a blonde teen in a tiny bikini I would never let my daughters wear. DeeDee took the cat for a walk, got lost, and a sympathetic police officer brought her directly to our door.

Jeff knew all the employees in the motel, and with the tacit approval of the cook he and Derek snuck into the restaurant kitchen to snatch goodies for late-night snacks. Marnie was disappointed that Scottsdale was a modern city, and Nikki had her first encounter with a cactus. Tweezers and sobs followed.

Finally we settled into our new home, five bedrooms and two baths with a heated diving pool. The kids were ecstatic. The boys joined baseball teams, the girls made friends in the neighborhood, and everything settled into a smooth routine. School would start in August, so the kids spent their time enjoying the rest of the summer. Funny, it was never too hot to go outdoors.

We had been in the house and Owen on the job for ten months when he came home one evening and announced he had lost his job in a layoff. He went through a lengthy explanation of how the semiconductor industry had taken a hit in a sluggish economy, and his new company along with many others was laying off hundreds of people.

He looked at me expectantly. I smiled sweetly and said, "I'm not moving again." ∼

Too Soon

Donna Bowring

Quiet surrounds me on this day. There are others here but I do not hear them, nor do I feel their presence. All I see is the black box sitting on a pedestal positioned in front of a row of wrought-iron benches. In front of the box sits a folded American flag.

A canopy shields us from the morning sun, but the June heat leaks its fingers into our hair and wraps itself around us. I feel myself beginning to melt. I picture myself as the Wicked Witch of the West with only my clothes left in a heap on the ground. I wish I could leave, wish I could tell everyone that there has been a terrible mistake.

We can all go home, I want to say, *he is not dead. Those are not his ashes in the black box on the pedestal in front of us. It is someone else. I am so sorry you had to come all the way out here for nothing.*

But it is too late. The chaplain is already here, the honor guard waits behind us, and the rifle guard stands at attention to one side waiting their turn to participate in this time-honored tradition.

My oldest son sits beside me. He says nothing but puts an arm around my shoulder as if to assure me that, should I need him, he is here. My other children sit behind me. My grandson babbles baby talk until his mother shushes him.

Under the clear blue Arizona sky, row upon row of markers stretch as far as the eye can see. There are small bouquets of flowers by some, and American flags decorate others. There are neat rake marks in the sand. Someone told me that as well as interments and placing of markers, caretakers trim the trees, take away the dead flowers, and rake and brush the markers clean every day.

A small breeze springs up as the chaplain shares the details of the deceased's life, gives a short homily, which my mind does not register. He recites a poem. I know I have heard the words before but cannot remember where. Perhaps in one of my literature classes.

Why am I trying to remember at this time where I heard a poem? The thought is probably a needed diversion. Something to keep my mind occupied so I won't have to think about saying goodbye.

I don't want to say goodbye; it is so final.

The Marine Honor Guard marches in stiff formation. Two men pick up the flag and begin the ceremonial unfolding and, when done, do a smart right turn, facing me while holding the fully unfurled flag. They turn to face each other again and fold the flag twelve times into its original triangle shape.

Another Marine marches forward and takes the flag from the other two. He takes two steps and kneels in front of me. *The President of the United States, the Marine Corps, and a grateful nation . . .* He goes on with the tribute given to all veterans whose final resting place is under the silent sand here in this serene, solemn place.

I look at him as he speaks. He is so young! My God, were we ever that young? Of course we were. Where did all the time go? The years slipped by without our counting them. We lived our lives as though we had forever to be together.

The young Marine places the flag in my lap, leans in, and says, "Semper Fi."

"Semper Fi," I whisper back. He smiles, stands and salutes, then is gone.

From off to the side comes the crack of rifles firing their final salute. A member of the guard marches to stand in front of me. She hands me the shells from the gun salute. They are still warm to the touch.

As she returns to formation, a bugler sounds Taps. As the notes drift into the morning air, we all stir. The ceremony is over; it is time for final goodbyes. I place my hand on the black box and bid my husband farewell.

"You went too soon," I tell him. ∾

The Road Less Taken:
Our Journey to Ghost Ranch

Ellen Buikema

The month of May arrived, and with it came time to plan our annual vacation. Every summer as a family we decided where we would visit. Since our girls were still in school these trips typically happened in August. Both daughters, Laurel and Julia, had a fondness for adobe structures and all things Native American, so we made the decision to head southwest. We would fly to Albuquerque.

Dave, an old friend from the university days and Methodist minister, had retired in New Mexico. Ralph, my husband, located Dave's phone number and reconnected with his friend from their Chicago days.

Ralph told Dave about our trip to Albuquerque and that we would bring our nine- and eleven-year-old daughters with us.

"Oh, that's the week I'll be in seminars at Ghost Ranch. I won't be home when you get in."

Sitting next to Ralph on the family room couch I overheard part of their discussion. At the mention of Ghost Ranch, I quickly got Ralph's attention. "Hold on. My wife's saying something." I reminded Ralph that I'd read about Ghost Ranch, near Abiquiu, up in the north central part of the state. One of my favorite artists, Georgia O'Keefe, had lived in and around Ghost Ranch. The area had inspired her quite a bit. It sounded magical to me. Ralph asked if Dave might have part of a day to spare.

"Sure! I'd love to see all of you. Let me know what day you plan to be here, and come on up!"

August is often hot and humid in the Chicago area. Stepping into the Albuquerque air brought relief. The sun was warm and the air dry with a light breeze. Perfection!

In a previous trip to Albuquerque we had discovered the joys of the Marble Cow, a marvelous place where one could mix any number of crunchy, chewy, delectable treats into an assortment of ice creams. It was bliss in a cup. The Marble Cow would be one of our first stops.

I have always enjoyed maps and disliked driving, so the role of navigator is often a natural given for me. This trip would prove to be a navigational challenge.

We drove through Sandia, Santa Ana, Zia, and the Jemez Indian Reservations to the little town of Cuba, New Mexico. There were two motels in Cuba; one billed itself as "The Friendliest Motel in Cuba." On the marque of the other motel we saw the words "The Cleanest Motel in Cuba."

To this day I don't know what we were thinking. We pulled into the parking lot of the "Friendliest Motel in Cuba." Indeed, the folks at the desk were very friendly. We were given a two-bedroom motel room for an excellent price. How could anything go wrong?

We entered the room. The closed blinds made it difficult to see. Reaching for the light switch, Ralph and I turned to see a very large room. Then we stepped on the carpet. This would be my first and hopefully last experience walking on a sticky carpet. I couldn't believe it.

"Girls, don't take off your shoes," we said simultaneously.

When we traveled, Laurel and Julia often were stuck sleeping in the same room with Ralph and me, since staying in motels can be expensive. They ran into what would be their own bedroom, relishing the privacy they would have from their parents. I'm sure the only thing that would top that would be the Marble Cow back in Albuquerque.

I checked out the bathroom, wincing as I walked across the gummy, flattened carpet. Despite the spaciousness of the bathroom, the tub frightened me. There were dark stains everywhere I looked. There was no way any of us would use that shower. The sink thankfully was not as stained and looked safe to use. We really should have left. I don't know if we stayed because Laurel and Julia were so deliriously happy about having their own room; perhaps we were too exhausted from the day. In any case we only stayed the night.

In the morning, our hosts smiled and waved to us as we departed. They really were very friendly.

After our sticky stay at the friendliest motel in Cuba I felt skeptical about the restaurants in town. Ralph reminded me that some of the best food can be found in out-of-the-way places, and it's not fair to judge a whole town on one motel. We drove off, looking for a promising restaurant.

On the main road in town, maybe a mile or two from the friendly motel, we saw a tiny diner. We were welcomed and asked to sit wherever we liked. We found a booth by the front window and made ourselves comfortable. Our waitress stopped by with water and menus.

After reading the descriptions of meals on the menu, Ralph and I chose huevos rancheros and coffee. Both girls chose French toast and juice. The coffee arrived first. I looked at it twice. Was this drinkable? It looked oily on the surface. Ralph and I requested fresh cups, pointing out that something seemed to be floating on the top of the coffee in front of us.

"Oh, sure, but that's just Cuba water," the waitress said pleasantly. "The next cup will look the same." She left with our cups and returned with new, steaming mugs of coffee. True to her word, the coffee had that same oily film on the top. It tasted fine, but I wonder about the effects that water had on the people who drink it daily.

The huevos rancheros were amazing, kicking off my love affair with green chiles. My taste buds were practically singing.

"Are you girls Girl Scouts?" asked the waitress. The girls answered yes, and we wondered why she had asked.

"Sometimes on Sundays the Girl Scouts come down from the mountain and eat here."

Come down from the mountain? What on earth was she talking about? We would find out soon enough.

After thanking our waitress for a wonderful meal, we went to find Dave. I had the atlas on my lap. We headed out of town on the main road, which became a highway just out of town, when suddenly we had to make a decision. Should we continue north and take Route 96?

"Let's take the scenic route. We need adventure driving," stated Ralph as I nervously looked at the map, hoping for the best.

The road, two lanes in both directions, was smooth as glass. Some miles down it narrowed. It became a one-lane road in either direction, still very nicely paved. I saw a sign that read, "Road closed in winter ten miles ahead." Well, it was summer. Why worry?

Then came the gravel.

Ralph is a terrific driver, so I was not overly anxious. Eventually the gravel became more and more sparse. Soon it was a two-lane clay road going on an upwardly route. Now I was anxious. At least we had filled the gas tank after leaving the restaurant.

The traffic was sparse going up the mountain. This was a good thing, as the two-lane winding mountain road became one-and-a-half car widths wide. Parts of the road on the driver's side, closer to the mountain, had clay-covered roots from massive pines jutting out onto the narrow road.

I was a mess. I was unable to relax and enjoy the beauty surrounding me. I was also on the side of the car closest to the drop-off. There was no railing on the roadside, just a few feet of earth, then a very steep, long way down.

Seeing that I was unusually quiet and obviously distraught, Ralph found a spot to pull over. He asked me to step out of the car with him. I reluctantly complied, nervously getting out of the car into the wilderness. Laurel and Julia had spent the entire drive either relaxing and reading or enjoying the view. Both girls remained in the car.

"Close your eyes and listen to the quiet," Ralph suggested in his calmest voice. "If you want to be able to enjoy the ride, you have to relax. Try it. Hear the quiet."

Not wanting to delay the trip and desperately wanting to finish this part of it, I closed my eyes and tried to quiet my mind. After I remembered to breathe, I listened to the breeze blowing through the pines, heard the birds singing to each other, and felt the warmth of the sun. Finally, I slowed my breathing and relaxed into the quiet. If Ralph had not suggested I do so, I do not believe I would have been able to enjoy our remaining time on the mountain in the Santa Fe National Forest.

We had seen yellow warning signs alerting us of cattle guards. We had no idea what cattle guards were and laughed, imagining cows standing upright with shotguns. We drove over metal grating that went across the road and discovered later that these were the cattle guards.

The road widened as we drove on. Looking to the right I saw a sign for the scout camp the waitress in Cuba mentioned. It was the first sign of any civilization. Farther down the road less traveled, we saw signs of domestic life: cows.

They were big. They were beautiful. They were blocking our progress.

Several brown cows decided to lie on the road. Both Laurel and Julia were intrigued. Ralph and I were not happy. We waited for a while, hoping the cows would move on their own. No such luck. We tried honking the horn. The cows looked at the car, chose to ignore us, and continued their siesta. We thought about inching forward, going around them if need be, and something about us moving motivated them to move too.

We passed by some beautiful homes set back close to the mountain. By this time we were in somewhat flatter terrain. Many of the homes had corrals with horses, some with cows. There was a tiny post office, then more traffic. Ralph was the first to notice Abiquiu Lake. It was much larger than I expected, blue reflected from the sky and dappled with sunlight. It was lovely.

We drove around a bend heading towards Ghost Ranch, and the subsequent view was like nothing I had ever experienced. Tears filled my eyes. To me, the area of Ghost Ranch was like a creative living being. The rocks curved, jutted, seemed to move with color, shape, cloud, and sun. I understood why this area drew artists. We drove past adobe buildings enclosed by low, curving walls.

We found Dave in one of the buildings. After we all hugged hello, I told him of my reaction to entering Ghost Ranch.

"Everyone feels differently," he told me. "There are some who say, 'You mean I drove all the way here for this?!' Others have a different sensitivity to the place. My wife and I love it here."

I love it too. ∿

Go Farther, Go Faster

Heather Cappel

My feet slip into the socks and shoes I laid by the bed last night. Getting everything ready ahead of time leaves me no excuses. I tie my shoes by the bare light over the toilet, eyes half closed and head heavy with sleep. My water bottle is by the front door on the counter sitting in a circle made by my headphone cord. I tie my key to my shoelace and set out, tennis shoes crunching over the pebbles that make up my typical Arizona lawn. The streetlamps are dimming and a pale light starts to spread across the rock-cut horizon. Today, I will run.

I never set out to start running. As a skinny, pale kid growing up in Oregon, I dreaded the spring when our PE class headed outside for track and field, on our route that went all around the school and began with a steep hill towards the pine-shaded neighborhood behind the soccer field. Inevitably, I was the farthest behind, even though once I'd gotten separated from the pack enough I would cut as many corners as I could just to make it back to the starting point before class was over, wheezing, face and chest red as blooming fireweed.

Lately I'd been getting fatter. It had been a year since I arrived fresh-faced and excited for a new job and a pretty rental house in the suburbs of Phoenix, a world away from the chilly and gray skies from my childhood. I moved here with a breathless eagerness to start my new life in sunny West Valley, certain that everything in my life was about to fall in place, ready to start a new life and erase the mistakes of my past.

I just started feeling settled in my newly suburban life when my mother got sick. Truth is, she'd been sick all along, struggling to reign in a sadness that had been swallowing her for years, attending Alcoholics Anonymous meetings, and reading and col-

49

lecting inspirational handbooks and pamphlets and workbooks. Her bookcases bent with the weight of them.

Sometimes these things helped her and she was sober and happy and painted brilliant bright watercolors filled with exotic plants and swirling colors.

Then she wrecked the car. Afterward, she disappeared for a week, hiding out with a friend in the country and drinking until the rest of her life was a fuzzy shape in the background of her mind. I called her once we found her. She was filled with grief and fear, apologizing through tears and promising to stay away so she didn't hurt anyone else. After this, she was never the same.

A few weeks later, I assigned her a special ring tone on my phone. It made an uncomfortably loud buzzing sound like a fire drill, so I'd know to be on guard when I answered. Her calls had gotten disturbing during the past few years, and as I settled into my new job in Phoenix the phone calls got worse. She'd call me crying in the afternoons. I'd take a cigarette break on the shipping docks outside of the gray industrial park office where I spent my days. I strained to hear her slurred words over the freight trucks idling.

She would call sounding hysterical, sentences and sobs spilling out of her, always reporting a new injury, how the bruises bloomed against her darker than ever before and how hard it was for any scratch to stop bleeding now, her blood getting thinner and thinner. I was angry. Five years ago her doctors said she'd be okay, if she took care of herself.

I'd come to the Southwest to escape the cold, but even as the sun overhead scorched my skin and burned my eyes, my heart grew frigid.

I developed insomnia. Boxes sat unpacked in the garage. My doctor could tell something was wrong when I came for a routine physical. I was pale and distracted; depression etched my features and weighed down my shoulders.

"We can help you with that," he said. "I can prescribe something for a while."

I thought of all the pill bottles in Mom's bedroom. There must have been hundreds of them stuffed into her nightstand drawers and cluttering the top of her bookcases.

"No drugs," I told him. "Maybe if I exercise more."

"Okay, sweetheart. That's a good plan." He nodded at me with a sympathetic smile and told me to make an appointment if I changed my mind.

So I started walking. I'd go out in the mornings before work just as the sun rose and before it got too hot.

I kept my headphones on, trying to feel the rhythm of the pavement. I thought of my Grand Papa who cheerfully walked every day of his retirement, fighting the good fight against diabetes only to lose shortly after his daughter lost her fight against darker demons.

I tried not to think. I felt my feet in my new cushioned shoes and concentrated on the feeling of landing on the ground below and bouncing off again. I timed my breathing to my music, sad and desperate songs written by dead junkies. I'd cry, right on the street, embarrassed to be seen by the kids racing each other on their way to the school bus and the old man on the riding lawnmower at the park who nodded at me with a little too much sympathy.

News from the family got darker and darker. Dad and I started talking more than we ever had. He'd call with news from rehabs, hospitals, mental wards. The sun was hot on my face as I sought the shaded side of the street for relief, and I could hear rain falling on his end.

"Don't know how much time we've got left. You haven't been around to see it, but these trips to the hospital are getting closer and closer together. When are you coming to visit?"

I went home just as the weather turned in Oregon. It was clear but too cold for walking. I stayed inside. I helped take Mom up the stairs when I was needed. Her swollen feet prevented her from walking and were wrapped in many layers of bandages and thick socks. I'd lift each heavy, padded foot to the next stair as my father held and guided her to the walker at the top, whispering encouragement in her ear with every painful shift of weight.

Coming down the stairs was a little easier. We bundled up in knit hats and blankets to huddle around the patio table and smoke too many cigarettes.

"I guess the cigarettes aren't going to kill me," she said with a chilly smile, staring at the glowing tip with yellowing eyes. "As long as I can keep enough blankets on me to keep from freezing to death might as well smoke."

I came back from the visit with a bad case of bronchitis. For three weeks I coughed and wheezed all through the night. I was still sick when I got the call. She died the Saturday after Thanksgiving after a long night of labored breathing.

I visited my doctor again before travelling back for her service, still wheezing and sick even after two rounds of antibiotics. He said I had asthma, probably always had, and raised his eyebrows at me for never knowing.

Stocked with a new inhaler, antibiotics, and a bottle of codeine cough syrup, I travelled home again for her memorial service away from the warm air and back to the chill of Oregon turning to winter.

It was December, much colder than my last visit, but now I *needed* to walk. It was the only thing that made me feel sane for a few moments. Still sick and dosing myself with codeine and my inhaler before I could get moving, I'd bundle up and struggle to breathe and keep moving. Images of my mother's face would flash through my mind and my heart would race, face flushed and lightheaded but going forward anyway, watching my shoes hit the wet ground and disturb the puddles, listening to the pulse in my temple and feeling the breath run out of my lungs.

I got a little better, but I still couldn't breathe right, so I kept up with the inhaler. In the spring, with the kind of logic that I assumed only the most screwed-up children of alcoholics could muster, I decided nothing would make me happy right now so I might as well quit smoking since I would be miserable either way.

I kept walking all this time, adding walks during my lunch hour and longer walks in the evening. It became my meditation.

The honeymoon period at my new job began waning, the hours grew longer, and the work piled up in uneven stacks on my desk. I'd be in a rage by lunchtime, nicotine deprived, mourning and full of self-pity, unable to tolerate either complaining or smiling. I put on thick headphones so no one would talk to me and took my lunch breaks to walk and get away.

I counted the empties along my path: down the industrial side street lined with flat walled factories and warehouses, to the train tracks crossing over at the pipe manufacturer with the fancy address sign made of welded pipes and fittings, and past the vast empty lot, filled with dry dirt, broken bottles, and squished empty cigarette packs.

Sometimes I'd forget my inhaler, and my breath would catch halfway through so I had to stop, bending over one of those bottles. I could imagine spending the night there, drinking my vodka and smoking a Camel Light. I couldn't get past the memories of hidden bottles and empty packs of smokes.

The only way to quiet my head was to go faster. I knew I couldn't run, but I couldn't help thinking of it: I imagined my breath slow and even, my legs pumping hard and fast. I decided to run anyway.

The first day I could only go fifteen seconds before I had to stop and wait a few minutes to catch my breath. I tried again, two days later. I ran a little longer, lost my breath again, just at the far edge of the park. I staggered the three blocks home, wheezing and embarrassed, cursing myself for forgetting my inhaler again. The next time I pulled my groin and nearly went crazy resting inside with my thoughts.

I kept trying, increasing my running intervals by tiny ten second increments. It got easier—barely.

Each time it takes my whole body and mind to run, just to keep control of my breathing and make my legs do the right movement so that I don't injure myself. When I run all my thoughts grow smaller and quieter until there is only breath and moving forward.

Nearly a year later, I ran my first mile straight through. Determined to reach some sort of milestone, I set the GPS tracker on my phone to tell me when I'd made it and then I let the forward momentum drive every other thought from my mind.

Heather Cappel

The spring sunrise light was perfect, casting a reddish desert glow against the stucco houses. My legs ached, and it felt like I was breathing fire. Finally, the voice came through my headphones: one mile completed. I survived, though my body ached, and I felt a smile unexpectedly forming on my face.

Next time I will go farther and go faster. ❧

A Book Cover

Eveline Horelle Dailey

The first draft of the manuscript was done. I paused to absorb the work and the emotions I experienced during the writing were finished. But then I remembered that the creator of the artwork for my other book covers was no longer available to me. My new book had no cover!

Creative I am, but resourceful I did not feel. Researching events, family matters, history, war, and so on had left me mentally drained. No compelling ideas came to mind, and the book cover continued to be blank.

I asked friends and foes for assistance. Most friends suggested that I paint a cover. I paint, yet the book in question with a title like "The Canvas" did not feel like a painting I needed to execute.

A window opened when an unlikely friend and former art student suggested that I contact the universities and the art schools in Arizona. A light went on, and I felt a glimmer of hope.

Using today's technology, researching the art departments of the various universities, colleges, and art schools was not difficult. Soon with names and email addresses on hand, I proceeded. The communication was simple. "I am a writer in need of a book cover." A good subject line, I thought, and continued with something like, "I am looking for an art student willing to work with me to create a book cover."

A professor told me that my correspondence would be posted so students would find what I was in need of.

When one is impatient the universe conspires to slow things to a crawl. I trust this to be a universal method to teach patience. It took about three weeks before I received the first email.

"I can work with you. I am very good. Attached is a contract you need to sign, and we will continue to communicate—

after you sign my contract."

Another email gave no semblance of credentials, but the person was clear in one area.

"How much are you willing to pay?"

I had about thirty solicitous emails, none of interest to me. I was discouraged, because unlike me these young artists had only their monetary benefit in mind. I was a writer, and my motivation was a need to write. Desperate, I did what an artist does: I got a canvas ready. My tools, tubes of paint, and brushes were also ready. I was not. The idea of creating my own cover in a painting sent me one more time to my computer. I needed a distraction, so I checked my emails.

"Hello. I read your post and would like to meet you. We can talk about what you have in mind, and perhaps I can work with you to create your book cover." The email was signed Ravit. A few emails later we decided to meet at a place convenient for both of us. My need for a good cup of soy cappuccino provided the rendezvous location.

I ordered my coffee, found a table facing the front door, and waited. I decided Ravit had to be a young man, basing my "scientific" assessment on the fact that only young men had responded to my inquiry. Again the universe conspired, guarding the door with my gaze. I counted fifteen young men coming through. No one appeared interested in me. Time slowed down again. A whole five minutes went by when a young woman, almost out of breath, opened the door. She walked directly toward me.

"Hi, I am Ravit."

That morning I had picked up my first iPhone from a vendor, and somehow I had sent it flying on a Saltillo floor. The glass cover shattered. Not a good omen, I thought, but I was there and so was this young woman. Something about her held my attention; even the omen suddenly seemed to mean something else. I offered her the chair next to me. Ravit sat. I offered her coffee or tea, and when she expressed no interest in either we began to talk.

"Tell me about your book."

Prepared with a short recap of the manuscript, living out

many details, I smiled at this head full of curls reminding me of my own head at that age. She looked attentive.

"A girl named Suzannah, the child of a Jewish doctor from Poland, moves to a small town in Germany where her father feels it will be best for the family, because they need a doctor in that town. Life takes an unexpected turn. Suzannah loses her parents and her older sister to the Nazi regime. Suzannah escapes and is found in the woods by a family of farmers. They bring her to safety.

"That is one important character in the book. The other, Julienne, born of an affluent French family, has a nanny. It is Suzannah. The adversities and horrors of WWII become topics of conversations. The years go by, and Suzannah becomes Julienne's friend, mentor, and a person who plays an unusual role in her existence. As life will have it, two succeeding events take her father and Suzannah out of the picture. After a series of confusing and turbulent incidents Julienne's life brings her to a new home in New England, a home left to her by her fairly new husband, an American professor who died in France.

"She embarks on the next phase of her life in the USA. Julienne knows no one, does not speak the language, and yet in this new environment a long porch, two rocking chairs, and a view of the harbor become her allies. She remembers the stories Suzannah told her. Her sorrow is followed by the courage to explore and go on, and Julienne discovers who she is."

When I finished talking she looked at me and without a word drew a small keyhole on a piece of paper. She must have been drawing all along. The drawing had advanced, and through the keyhole I could see a rocking chair and seven steps Julienne had to climb.

"Your book has a secret."

When I had originally begun to write, I called my book *The Canvas.* That day after meeting Ravit, I added the subtitle *A Secret from the Holocaust.*

The laws of intuitive attraction were favoring me when I met Ravit. Within three days I had my book cover. This young artist had captured the essence of the manuscript, and as an artist myself I found her to be awesome.

A year later I collaborated on a book with Dr. Gladys Mc-Garey MD, MD(H). She is a Medical Doctor and a Doctor of Homeopathic Medicine, and we needed a book cover. We wanted something special, and I suggested Ravit as the cover artist.

"So where does she comes from? She does not have an American name," Dr. McGarey asked.

I now know that the name "Ravit" is a rich cultural soup that began to boil in the heart of Poland a long time ago, perhaps during the same timeline that Suzannah's family left their land to move to Germany. Ravit's family immigrated to Morocco, and before there was a country called Israel they moved to Jerusalem where many decades later a baby girl named Ravit was born in Israel.

In retrospect, I feel the glass particles of a broken iPhone were the omen that opened new doors for me to penetrate. These particles reflected Ravit's face for the universe to watch and for me to smile about. The universe provided me with more than a person drawing book covers; I met an individual to watch as she grows and makes her own way in the world. ∾

I Met A Master

Eveline Horelle Dailey

For my own good, I was told the hard labor inflicted upon me would enhance whatever gray matter could be found in my head. Looking back I appreciate the exchanges my teachers had. They discussed the sciences and the arts that would render me a well-rounded free adult. With their pronouncement, a great deal of homework followed. I found it impossible to reason with these tutors.

A young girl ready to dance with life and Elvis Presley emerged from my torments. To boogie and rock and roll, I had to convince my family of good reasons to journey to America.

I left the tarmac with languages other than English. I took my first steps in the U.S., and the first impression was dreadful. College bound, parents with intentions similar to my old teachers, art and science would be my focus. No one cared or appreciated my wish to dance with Elvis.

The land of the free did not offer me what I expected. Invincible and knowing all things, I did not foresee or look forward to instructions delivered in the language of the land. I did not understand English, and this fact was not sufficient to change the reality that I was stuck in a place where nothing made sense. Resigned and given no choices, I went to school, forgot about my idol, and soon enough words began to flow. My heart opened, and I began to enjoy the lessons. The teachers penetrated the gray matter.

These formative years came with the stuff that would make me a woman able to appreciate the arts and the adventures they would provide. The universe was pleased and took over. An *Arizona Highway* magazine at a doctor's office in New York provided me with a stepping-stone to another phase of my life.

I could feel the beauty in each page. The clarity of colors and the shades and shapes of the landscape and the sky were mind-altering. Ambers and reds and greens so pale the bushes were almost gray. Clay-like formations held my attention, and my soul responded. My eyes and senses wanted more. I understood the art and the science of a master craftsman.

The complicated emptiness brought by a failing marriage could be filled by what I had seen on the pages of this magazine; I felt it in my bones. Freedom, as I understood it, did not happen by the simple movement of a wand, yet I knew boulders and mountains made of clay would show me the way.

I vaguely remembered an article I read in an issue of *Paris Match*. The article told about the civil rights movement, freedom, and a sculptor named John Henry Waddell who was returning home from a stay in Mexico. Waddell was indignant because in his country four young girls had to die because they were black.

The article stated that this man would create a work in the medium he knew. The sculpture would be dedicated to the four children in Alabama who died during a bombing in a church. Not familiar with all aspects of American affairs, I understood that this man knew something about the expression of freedom. The pictures in this magazine in the doctor's office summoned thoughts of words I had read long ago.

A head full of colors, boulders, mountains of clay, and sounds of streams became the objects of my paintings, but something else neatly placed in a compartment far away in the caches of my mind lingered.

My life, however empty, was safe. The big house complete with a white picket fence, a German sports car, and daughters were not enough to stop a longing I could not explain. My impressionist paintings could not capture what was too subtle to brush on a canvas.

I had to move to Arizona.

I had a diluted idea about freedom and my personal civil rights. I understood the principle but had no practice in matters of freedom or civil rights, whatever they were. I was a wife, a mother, a painter, a designer, and all was in order.

It was after the move from New York in the desert of Arizona that expression took form. A rattlesnake and a strange, menacing creature named a Gila monster became my next set of teachers. Neither discussed art or science with me. I came to understand my personal freedom, and I attached it to the word "run." Understanding came after a mile of panic-stricken flight.

I was afraid of things unfamiliar.

Metaphors and catalysts continued to fill my life. The monster and the snake were the deciding factors propelling my transformation. Higher elevations where the summer heat was a few degrees less than what I had experienced in the Valley of the Sun became the next destination. The pages of my stolen magazine came alive in a town called Sedona. It held another phase of my story. Destiny continued the choreography of a dance. Surrounded with art and artists exploring their potential and trying to understand their reason for being, I began to meet the most remarkable people.

One was the founder of Gardens for Humanity, an organization planting gardens in places of need. Schools, prisons, and Indian reservations became my playgrounds. I knew nothing about planting but was granted a different kind of adventure to experience. I was in another classroom where the opened door was the language of my heart.

Now, decades later, I can say the founder of this organization, Adele Seronde, is one of the most remarkable people I have ever met. She knew intimately the sense of freedom I was still searching for. This woman got me mixing manure and mulch, planting seeds with school children. For me "normal" was becoming something else; it became evident that the manipulation of earth and seed was transforming something within me. In the process it was not only flowers or vegetables that bloomed, it was me.

The adventure continued; an art gallery soon followed. I was a free agent able to follow the commands of my destiny. Freedom looked a lot like the Arizona sunset I loved, sure to happen yet different every day. One day, Adele suggested, we visit

John. Another artist, another show. Why not?

"You drive. It is a difficult road to the studio in Cornville."

The drive *was* difficult on a dirt road with enough rocks to make many boulders. Suddenly without warning in the top left of my periphery, there was a sculpture looking at me; her hands extended as if to tell me to drive on. Soon another sculpture appeared by some desert trees. She was dancing. I do not know when I stopped the car.

"You just entered the sculpture garden; you will love it!" Adele said.

Paris Match came to mind; the article had been about an American sculptor named John. Could it be?

"Adele, is this the work of sculptor John Henry Waddell?"

"Well, yes. I do not know any other John."

We drove a bit more, and this time I parked the car nearly in the open arms of a volcano.

"Perfect timing, you two." A man in the full regalia his foundry demanded welcomed us. "Ruth just prepared a salad, and we are going to eat by the creek." In my car I had some groceries that had not made it home. Chocolate from Belgium, some French bread, a piece of Brie cheese large enough to share. Miracle!

John took my hand, put the groceries on a bench, and led me to the studio. He was working on a series of dancers for a bas-relief. They were installed on a whitewashed wall, probably 75 feet tall. The figures were alive and dancing; they were made of wax.

"Soon they will be casted."

On the floor life-size sculptures of men and women, graceful nudes, drew me in. On the windowsills smaller sculptures continued to entice my eyes. My new friend John explained the processes necessary to produce the sculptures. We talked about each work I pointed to. He was generous with his time and answered each question I had. We continued to walk to different rooms, and between steps I decided I would come back again. This place was a magnet to my soul.

We went to another room. This one had shelves, floor to ceiling on one side, and two tall ladders to procure what treasures were stashed inside the shelves. Taller shelves were filled with a variety of ceramic pieces. The bronzes had brought me to a state of awe; moments later paintings demanded that I pay a different type of attention. I saw wonderful watercolors of the Grand Canyon, of his wife, Ruth, and his children. Works of ceramic were equally important. I was in the studio of a man with more than one art form and evidently one who had mastered the art of living. I smiled inside where no one could see.

From the corner of my eye, taped on the wall, I saw a piece of newspaper, an article similar to the one I had read in *Paris Match*. This one was in English, and the title was "That Which Might Have Been." There was a photo next to the article. The article I had read talked of the four children I had read about, but the picture was of four adult women.

"Mr. Waddell, I would like to see these, because when I was a young mother I read about why you decided to sculpt the four children that were killed in Alabama."

"Have you achieved a degree of mental and spiritual freedom?" he asked me as he showed me a larger-than-life a mother and child. He did not respond to my request.

John Henry Waddell became a good friend, and every year to celebrate the new year his work adorned the art gallery. *The Mother and Child* was the first sculpture to enter the gallery. *That Which Might Have Been* was not.

To see this installation I had to go to the Unitarian Universalist Church on Lincoln Drive and 40th Street in Paradise Valley in Arizona. The statues of four Negro women showing strength they did not have time to express as children can be seen and felt there. At the time of the pouring, *That Which Might Have Been— Birmingham 1963* was not acceptable in Alabama.

Despite the fact that the sculptures were not acceptable in Alabama, their spirit and what they implied long ago continue to be important. It is evident that in Arizona I achieved a degree of mental and spiritual freedom. ❧

The Inipe

Eveline Horelle Dailey

A turn from the highway brought me to a small town. The embracing markers to my adventure were an antique store, a bar, and a gas station. Nothing seemed remarkable as I continued the drive toward Lake Montezuma where the water is 78 degrees and cliff dwellings from a long gone Indian tribe surround the park. Nature, history, and anthropology all in one—I could not ask for better.

It was a cold December day, and the vegetation was mostly dormant or dead. The taller shrubs stood like golden goddesses awaiting something I missed. To my left I noticed a small building with an artistic sign telling me about jewelry inside. I had lived in many capital cities, and no jewelry store I had seen had this particular appearance.

A quick U-turn was in order. There was something inviting about the oddity of the place. The lone parking space was available to the store seemingly made for one. My refrigerator looked larger than the entire building. The front door, made of a variety of woods, did not appear able to secure anything of consequence. Surprisingly, it was heavy. I opened it.

One light inside allowed me to see the most incredible treasures, covering shelves of various sizes. Pleased with my discovery, I noticed no one seemed to be around so I took my time examining one-of-a-kind pieces of art, rings, bracelets, necklaces, and so on. Exquisite pottery decorated with turquoise, copper, and antlers stood as guards on a corner of the store. My eye rested upon objects I had never seen before.

A back door I had not noticed opened, and a man well-seasoned by the sun came in smiling.

"I see you found Alpha Centauri. Welcome!"

He noticed I was looking at a particular silver pendant I could not reach. Without a word he handed it to me.

"This is an exquisite piece of jewelry," I said. "Do you know who made it, and how much it is?"

I examined every inch of this piece of art and decided it belonged on my chest. I could almost feel the force it took to create the grooves where the silver was left unpolished. The artisan had inserted pieces of turquoise and coral in a long channel. The impression was one of a necktie.

The man smiled and told me he made the piece, and he would gladly sell it to me. He opened another door, and without wasting a breath he asked me if I wanted to see where he worked. Soft music I had not heard in the showroom was playing. *A friendly fellow,* I thought. I followed him.

I had never seen how gold, silver, and stones were transformed to become wearable art. He showed me the wax of a ring he was creating. A customer wanted to give the ring to his wife for their anniversary. He explained the various processes he used and what the ring would look like.

The interaction with this man took minutes, and I told him I would be back to purchase the pendant still in my hand. We agreed on a price, and I left.

"By the way, my name is Christopher, and I will keep this for you. See you down the road."

Lake Montezuma and the cliff dwellings were not a difficult trek, because the forest and park people had prepared trails for people like me. I was puzzled, in awe, and very cold. I met a woman who showed me the various caves. She was Lakota; Susan was the name she gave me. It was a good afternoon to chat, but I was getting progressively colder. I decided to head back home where I controlled how warm I could be.

The new year approached, and so did my birthday. I made a mental note to return to the store no later than Thursday. In my living room, a glorious fire I had started kept me warm. I could see the creek that detoured on my property. The temperature was dropping, and the usual creatures outside had taken shelter. I sat by the fire with my dogs and read Rumi.

Two days later, I went back to the store ready for my pendant. Christopher did not take credit cards; too complicated, he told me. He was lucky I had my checkbook with me.

We talked a short while, and he asked me if I wanted to go on a "sweat." He noticed my surprise.

"An American Indian friend will be here in a short while. We are having a sweat tonight to honor Grandmother. My friend is giving his wife her present. I finished it; let me show it to you. We each bring something to share. We all like hot foods. What about you? Wear cotton. I am the fire keeper, and the lodge is on my property."

My new friend talked nonstop without taking a breath. The door opened. A woman entered and told Christopher she would rush home and finish the chili. In seconds she was gone. This small place had a dynamic quality to it and was obviously full of life. The door opened again. This time a man close to seven feet tall and as wide as the doorway entered. His hair was black and in a ponytail. A woman was with him. He was a Native American; she was not.

"Hello, I am Bear's wife. Are you sweating tonight? I don't recall ever seeing you before."

Remembering my mother telling me that ladies did not sweat, they perspired, I told her I was not going to sweat.

"Just in case, Christopher, why don't you give your friend the directions to your place? Bring something we all can eat, and wear cotton. See you up the hill."

They left. Christopher handed me a piece of paper with a drawing and a phone number in case I got lost. I left too and, once at home and wearing my new jewel, I gave this sweat thing some thought. It was a cold winter night, and some people talked about sweating. I could think only of one thing: no one sweats in this weather.

I walked my dogs wearing my coat, scarf, gloves, hat, and boots. Once back home I eyed the large pot of vegetable soup I had made the day before. I could bring that. I would add some curry or pepper and make it hot.

Cotton. I wondered why they said to wear cotton. Who wears cotton when it is freezing outside?

Before long, I was wearing a pair of loose cotton pants, a heavy pair of cotton socks, and a cotton shirt. I was ready to go. I put the pot of soup in the car and put my snow jacket on. With my piece of paper in hand, I headed to a mountain in Rimrock where the roads are not paved and there are no streetlights. The directions were not bad, the moon was full, and I could see the various markers as they came upon me. Up and down trails rather than roads, my light beams collaborated and I finally made it. It was windy and cold. There were about six cars in the driveway. I proceeded toward the front door. The pot of soup was heavy. A light went on and I noticed the front door, a work of art. I made a mental note to ask Christopher about it.

A Chinese woman opened the door, immediately hugged my neck, and invited me in. She showed me her new ring and told me she would have to take it off before entering the Inipe. I had no one to ask what an "Inipe" was but gathered I had to take my rings off. No one told me why.

I was stuck with a group of people I did not know and about to enter a thing called an Inipe, and I did not know what that was. A dozen people around a dining room table were chatting with the Bear. They must have been waiting for a sign. Apparently I was not it.

"We are making ties. Here, sit, I'll show you what to do."

Square of colored fabrics fanned out all over the center of the table along with the brightest yellows, greens, reds and other colors. String and small bowls with tobacco and sage and other herbs I could smell but did not know also dotted the table. A larger bowl held ground corn. In a basket there were pieces of soft leather. Those were to make "bundles," my Chinese friend told me, but I was not ready for that. Special sweet herbs and good intentions went inside the bundles.

I was lost in a world I did not know existed; the chatter was incessant and punctuated with laughter. The oddity of my life came to mind. I was different from these folks, yet there was an element of ease that surprised me.

Next to me, a small woman looking much like a bird began. "You take a square, put a little tobacco or a little herb, and you tie it. See, like this. Then you start all over again. We tie them to the ribs of the Inipe."

That word again, and it had ribs! With great difficulties I made some "ties." Christopher was nowhere to be found. I asked about him, and a man told me he was the fire keeper so he was up . . . wherever "up" was.

Soon enough, it was time to walk to the Inipe. I must have missed the sign. At this point all I could do was follow or get back in my car and go home. I chose to follow the leader—Bear. The temperature outside was in the twenties, and it was only 9:00 P.M.

We walked toward a raging fire. Each person took his or her coat and shoes off and entered a round structure covered with large and numerous blankets. A special blanket doubled up as a doorway.

Christopher was taking care of the fire. The fire pit was red with rocks larger than my head. Some were so hot they were blue. All coat and shoes lay on the ground not too far from the fire.

I understood the sign and the cue. I took off my coat and shoes and put them the closest to the fire, but I kept my socks on. My body went into shock. It was the coldest I had ever experienced with an incessant breeze. I entered the Inipe. Now I knew what this structure was called, and it had its own fire pit. Rocks similar to the ones in the fire pit outside were in the center. It was very comfortable, probably seventy degrees.

I was getting less anxious as I decided on a spot. The flap opened, and a gust of cold wind changed everything. Christopher delivered more rocks. All along, people took time to say their names. Some talked about rather personal things. When it was my turn, I was given a feather. I gave my name and added the fact that I had no idea what I was doing there. The Bear laughed.

"I am sure you will find out. Sometimes Grandmother is ready to reveal things to her grandchildren, and if you are here and don't know if you are coming or going there is a reason. You will find out."

I was petrified and could feel my body stiffening and also trembling. I think my eyes got bigger. I noticed the Inipe was held together by a series of bent wood branches. The flap opened again, and Christopher delivered more rocks. It was no longer seventy degrees but more than a hundred. There were about thirty rocks. I asked my neighbor how many rocks would be making their appearance in the pit. She explained that tonight would not be a full sweat, because it was Jane and Ralph's anniversary.

Now I knew both their names. I was very uncomfortable. More rocks and then more rocks. I counted fifty-two—one for each week of the year. I was glad they did not count days of the year with their rocks. I questioned their sanity and mine for being there.

Something strange was going on. My skin seemed to have been losing a layer or two of itself. I was cooking from the outside in. I was certain of it. I also was very thirsty. I guess when one is cooking one needs basting. I was glad the woman had told me about the rings, because my fingers would have been crisp and covered with liquid gold.

People kept talking about their lives, and I kept thinking I was among a group of insane people. It was difficult to accept that I had volunteered for this ordeal. A woman spoke, and I recognized the voice. It was Susan, the Lakota woman from Lake Montezuma. Somehow I missed her around the table, or perhaps she was the fire keeper's helper. She began singing in her native language, a rhythmic series of sounds or words. Bear followed, and the rest of the group said some words I did not know. I was roasting.

"We are all family, and we are all one."

I do not know who was talking, but family or not something was happening to me. I was sweating, not perspiring, and I thought of my mother. I laughed. Bear's wife asked me why I was laughing, and I told her. Bear told me I was family and told us all it was time to go back inside and share a meal. I was no longer a prisoner inside an Inipe.

We put our shoes and coats on and walked back down from the mountain into the house. This time Christopher was with us. We shared a meal, and I was invited to come the next time at full moon. Grandmother would like that.

Something did happen to me. I experienced a great deal of joy around that table, and the camaraderie I felt was incredible. The group knew one another at a level I had not experienced. The people I knew or members of my family did not share what went on inside. They obviously had never been to a sweat! These people treated me as if I had always been with them, although I thought they were all insane. Perhaps I was insane.

I spent about two years going to "sweats," entering the Inipe with my ties of sweet herbs and tobacco. I shared stories, emotions, and meals with people who had become family. And one day Bear said some of us were ready for a Vision Quest. I had mastered sweating, made some bundles of fine leather and fringes. I was not sure of what I would do next. ∞

In the Presence of Royalty: A Memoir

John Daleiden

Our June 2007 move from Midwestern Iowa to the Phoenix Sonoran Desert spurs an extreme experience in comprehending change. I reach the conclusion the only constant factor in human lives is change. Nothing in life remains static—nothing in life stays the same. We base our entire move on that premise.

> *the "things" we owned*
> *sorted and packed in boxes—*
> *loaded on a van . . .*
> *headed southwest, a new life*
> *in the Valley of the Sun*

Unsure if we will like life in this new environment, prior to our move we rent a one-bedroom apartment in a large complex complete with two swimming pools. On the day we arrive in Avondale, the moving company notifies us the delivery of our furniture is delayed one week. We both sigh. With stalwart determination, we trek to the nearest mall so we can purchase necessary goods to make life in a bare apartment tolerable. We spend $150.00 on essentials like a blowup mattress, one change of bed linens, a set of two plates and cheap silverware, two mugs, and an electric skillet. We resign ourselves to live a Spartan life— this was not the first time we had to live in a frugal manner.

Instead of one week, our furnishings arrive 25 days late— three weeks and four days. The moving company somehow temporarily lost our possessions. Fortunately the movers located them, only to discover everything is on a truck headed to Portland, Oregon. Our goods have taken the vacation to the Northwest coast we could not afford. The mover notifies us our "stuff" will arrive on Saturday, July 14, 2007.

John Daleiden

On the appointed day, two burly movers unload and set up the furniture in our first-floor apartment. They are cordial and do not complain when my wife and I ask them to relocate several of the larger items not just once, but twice!

> *Spartan life*
> *in a bare apartment ends—*
> *the movers arrive . . .*
> *as each box is opened,*
> *we discover old treasures*

Life has a way of going on just like the turning hands on the face of a clock, moving at an infinitely slow pace second after second, minute after minute, hour after hour. The hours become days, the days complete weeks, and soon months pass.

My wife begins her new teaching job as a special education teacher in a local middle school. Her stories about the new staff and new procedures entertain me and sound familiar. All these changes in Deborahanne's professional life look similar to the changes in our domestic life.

Frustration seems to be a natural outcome of experiencing change. We encounter aggravations: Deborahanne in her professional life as a local Phoenix educator and both of us in our marriage relationship. I become analytical of my annoyances. I recognize a need to put matters into a proper perspective.

Boundaries

> *Paths*
> *lead*
> *beyond*
> *the meadow*
> *through ominous woods.*
> *I walked there yesterday past dark*
> *entanglements, dense spider webs fraught with the black*
> *corpse*
> *of my now-discarded demons,*
> *shed when fear threatened*

to consume
my acts
once
moral

An
edge
of doubt
restored faith
on my short journey—
yesterday, in the darkest hour
I thought of never seeing your bright eyes at breakfast—
each morning, sipping hot coffee,
observing weather, and small talk—
those words
we speak
all
day
never
hearing what
has been left unsaid—
without hesitation I knew
that if we continued to race downward on that path,
the entanglements and thickets
of deceit would kill
our garden
with lies
and
fear.

We put aside
the cankers,
dark impediments,
and permit only the blue skies
of deep passions to guide us where we walk hand in hand.

The move to Phoenix separated us physically from our
32-year-old unmarried son who has lived independently since

John Daleiden

he was 16 years old. At the time of our move, Matthew lived in Des Moines, Iowa. Since our Oskaloosa, Iowa, home was only 60 miles from Matthew's Des Moines home, we could easily visit each other. Suddenly, Matthew was more than 1,000 miles away from Phoenix.

Shortly after our move, Matthew becomes engaged to a lovely young woman who is also a special education teacher. They intend to marry on August 8, 2008—08-08-08, an auspicious date. We look forward to this marriage with fervor.

The couple invites me to say a few words on their behalf at the nuptial celebration. I write my wedding remarks three weeks before the celebration, polish and hone them, and memorize the speech. Several days prior to the wedding, we board a plane to Iowa for the first time since the move. However, once we are airborne the text suddenly seems wrong. I spend the seven flight-and-layover hours composing a new text. I am in a mild state of panic. After reviewing my epithalamium the next day, I am completely satisfied.

On Your Wedding Day

For Sara and Matthew Herrin on 08-08-08

I weep tears of joy this night as you wed, son.
Such bright gems—silent beauty—together, repeating
your vows.
The lily and bronze hibiscus—grand, radiant, and regal.

The love path is fraught with curves, disappointment,
and great pleasure.
Marriage races like mountain streams—hot, cold, in tor-
rents and eddies.
Take her hand and walk unified through dark days into
the light.

Listen to the world in pain, and speak to each other of love.
Drink lustily at the well of human flesh—know each other.
Once each night clasp your precious hands in loving trust—
quiet joy.

I am astounded when two hundred-plus wedding guests applaud. Later in the evening when we are alone in the hotel room, I hand my wife a second poem I wrote on the flight. She asks me to read aloud. I do not have to read from her printed copy. I speak these words from my heart:

The Healing

Drink hot tea with me tonight—we'll watch the moon light dark shadows.
Tell me your secrets and fears—I'll listen with forgetfulness.
The sad songs of old transgressions disappear when our lips touch.

We return to Phoenix. Immersed in the events of daily life we enjoy reports from our son and daughter while they honeymoon in Jamaica. The late August heat of the desert is relentless. For diversion, we join another couple from Deborahanne's school for a Saturday tubing trip on the Salt River. We have much fun and experience a pleasant respite from the torturous summer desert temperatures. We both contemplate our journey through life as we age:

. . . As Time Goes By . . .

Our bodies grow old and our hair turns gray;
quickness in our steps is slowed and labored,
but our hearts are filled with joy each new day.
Are we now different? How have we been changed?

Each fine morning I say you have not aged;
we read news and drink tea at the café.
I speak of this and that like a graybeard—
our bodies grown old and our heads turned gray.

Once we thought we were made of sterner clay—
Rock-hard stuff mined from a far mountain range,
then fired in a red hot forge every day—
now, our quickened steps are slowed and labored.

You, my brown beauty, shaking your tabor,
singing love songs—such a tasty soufflé—
loving naively in a green arbor—
then our hearts were filled with joy each new day.

This morning, dining in the cabaret,
you tell me life makes you feel stale and caged—
smoke surrounds you—I call you Lady Day . . .
Why are we different? Tell me how we changed?

You say, life is a sharp, deadly saber—
I say, time is like every man's valet . . .
a caring mover, a waiting neighbor
bearing an ancient, delicate bouquet
of bodies grown old . . .

We celebrate our first Thanksgiving and Christmas without children. Phone calls via Skype replace our physical presences with them. In their absence, we cultivate friendships with various teaching colleagues and musicians who live and perform in the valley. On New Year's Eve, we host a grand costume party. Mickey Mouse, Snow White, and several Dwarfs arrive to herald the new year. Deborahanne wears the costume of Christina, and I don the mask and cape of her pursuing Phantom. Shortly after midnight Matthew and Sara phone to tell us we will become the grandparents of a girl. I am not sure who is more thrilled—the parents-to-be or the expectant grandparents.

While We Wait

ninety-four days
with not a drop of rain
in this spring desert—
thank God we still make love
after forty-three years!

in morning sun
the ancient saguaro
a-twitter with song—

my little bird, rest a while
by my side in this warm bed

do you think this gray
in my hair is becoming?
yesterday, I cried
when my sister telephoned
to say her marriage ended!

our first grandchild
will be born in a few days!
how old we are now—
distant is the memory
of his pre-mature birth

listen to the wind—
perhaps the rains come today!
hold my hand please—
how tiresome, watching sand
trickle through the hourglass

red sky at sunset—
expecting sailor's delight
I trim my sails
perhaps our passions will meet
in perfect harmony

In late spring Victoria Ann Herrin is a healthy baby upon her arrival at 5:23 A.M. in Des Moines, Iowa. She weighs 7 pounds, 11 ounces and is 20.5 inches long. There is no more adorable child in the entire nursery. Mother Sara Rae is fine, and her husband, Matthew Shawn, cannot stop smiling. An era has rushed through a newly opened door in all our lives.

Pain and trouble in life often follow joy. On June 29th fire strikes fear in the hearts of high-country Arizona dwellers. An abandoned campfire starts a devastating blaze. The Wallow fire event causes the evacuation of more than 6,000 people. Firefighters achieve one hundred percent containment at 6 P.M., July 8. The fire burns more than 538,000 acres, destroys 32 residential structures, 4 commercial structures, and 36 outbuildings. It costs more than $79 million to fight. Grim pictures dominate every evening television news broadcast.

Caught in the Path

in the high country—
beneath billowing clouds
a pleasant day

mountain retreat—
Bear Wallow Wilderness scorched
with wild fires

three P.M.
the sheriff orders us
from our homes

on the fire line
air tankers dump retardant—
a burned out home

fleeing in cars
loaded with possessions—
smoke obscures the road

setting back fires
to clear the forest floor—
a night sky at noon

all cots taken
at the refugee gym
a baby cries

in the rubble
a signed picture smeared with ash—
the chimney remains

bare, charred trees
stand on the mountainside—
the scent of scorched pine

foot prints in the ash

we leave our memories
to a blue sky day

. . . And down in the valley urban life goes on—the familiar scenes of daily life repeat themselves with interesting variations.

all day
riding the Metro Light Rail—
a homeless man

on every block
new for sale signs—
foreclosure paradise

waiting, waiting
on the six-lane freeway
a beggar walks by

red lights flashing
in the rearview mirror—
nowhere to stop

. . . the Metro Light Rail. The jammed-up freeways. Emergency vehicles rushing from place to place. The ever-present foreclosure and for sale signs. All familiar objects and conditions in our urban landscape but also charged with lively variation. Is there nothing in our lives that is constant? Are we surrounded only by change and the relentless thrust of time? We both long for quiet contentment. We yearn for the familiar, the predictable, and the known.

In the Valley of the Sun

Visions
cloud our mad minds—
we seek shelter from strife
in a saguaro's slim shadows
at noon.

Yucca
blooms bend in winds
from distant mountain peaks;

soaring on thermals, two golden
eagles.

—the night,
alive with sounds,
whispers on sandy winds—
ti-pi-ya-oh, call the drovers
voices.

Full moon—
a coyote
slinks through thick, dark mesquite;
in the distance the Estrella
Mountains.

At dawn
a glint of light
reflects in each broad curve
of Gila River—the crops lush
and green

Somehow, Phoenix, Arizona, has become our home. The desert landscapes make imprints in our minds. Although we just returned from Iowa, that once-familiar rolling countryside did not seem like home any longer. We laugh about the fact that we exchanged Iowa winter snow for 110-plus summer Arizona heat. In the snow I had to shovel for many hours each time a blizzard blanketed the land; in Arizona, when it got hot, all I had to do was turn on the air conditioner and sweat a little. My cardiologist claims I made a wonderful, lifesaving trade.

In August 2010 we purchase a new home, a two-story, three-bedroom house in southwest Phoenix. For about two months we stay very busy acquiring new furnishings and settling into spacious quarters. The temporary rental of a two-bedroom apartment in Avondale gave us time to locate a property where we feel certain we can retire completely when the time comes.

Life is an adventure. Part of the adventure is rediscovering the love of my life.

In the Stillness at Sunrise

Haitian woman,
spawn of powerful genes—
work your spell
use your voodoo fingers
to enliven this old man

like the climbing rose
let my arms encircle
your brown torso
whisper in my ear
to make me bloom

electrify me—
spin your youth in a charm,
awaken runes
dormant with age and distance,
refresh our dwindling lives

In the morning
we rise and part for work—
each day is full
the chocolate morsel at lunch
swells my thought of your delights

in the mid-day heat
undesirable plants grow
with great passions
I cultivate our tidy
garden, clipping spent blooms

feed our bodies—
extraordinary cuisine
with delicate skill
your specialties quell hunger
and still our wondering souls

cricket song at dusk . . .
the charcoal smell of salmon

John Daleiden

fills my senses
beside you in firelight
all my longings vanish

together we thrash
as though in a rip tide—
clinging to the edge
of being, we reach a shore
touching the cooled sands again

spent, side by side—
we watch spilled stars brighten
in velvet blackness
can you ever know the depth
of my love for you?

frayed brown grasses
dormant in the morning sun—
the call of a crow
in the stillness at sunrise
I kiss your bare shoulder

when I die
mould an amber amulet
with my ash
wear it around your neck
dangling in your brown breasts

The beauty of Arizona has spurred me to discover two wonders on my own street: I share life with a queen and poetry is the queen of language. ∾

Failure of the Heart in the Valley of the Sun

Bob Duckles

I sit at my kitchen table in Phoenix, Arizona. I feel fine. I am relaxed. At the same time, I know if I try to do anything—just stand up and walk out to the garage to unload the car—I will be gasping for breath.

"I'm recovering from surgery" has been my standard answer when asked, "Are you okay?" but I've been recovering from surgery for three weeks. Yesterday it took me forever to make the bed. One flight up the stairs in the parking garage had me winded.

"You don't look so good," my wife, Patricia, says. "You look pale. Maybe you should call a doctor."

I slip my portable oximeter on my finger. My oxygen saturation is 96 percent. Good. My pulse is 135. Very high. I remove and replace the oximeter several times. The reading stays the same.

I don't want to feel foolish if this is nothing. It becomes clearer it is something. I find my pulmonologist on my phone's speed dial. Her service answers. I describe my symptoms. She returns the call in less than two minutes. I give her the data from my oximeter. She tells me to get to an emergency room.

I am suffocating. I can't breathe. Is this what waterboarding feels like? I lie on my back on a bed sliding me into the donut hole of the CAT scan machine. I desperately want to sit up. I am about to crawl out of the bed.

"Lie still. You don't need to hold your breath." That's good. They must know I could not do it. My upper body heaves as I try to suck air into my lungs. I feel like there is no air.

When I can sit up, it helps. I am still short of breath, panting, but I don't feel as desperate as I did. I am returned to the hospital bed, and the head is raised as high as it will go. I look at my monitor. Heart rate is 136. Oxygen absorption is 95 percent. How can that be? How can I have so much trouble breathing and still have oxygen absorption in my blood at normal levels?

Sitting in my bed, I am wheeled back to my curtained cubicle in the emergency room. I blow out through pursed lips to clear carbon dioxide from my lungs to make room for oxygen-laden air, which I breathe in through my nose. This helps. My oxygen absorption stays the same: 95 percent. My pulse is still 135.

I have been in the emergency room for more than an hour before I am given my diagnosis: atrial fibrillation. The upper right chamber of my heart is beating out of sync with the rest of my heart. It is serious for, among other reasons, the danger of blood clotting when it pools in the atrium instead of moving on. The clots can then move to the lung, impairing an already compromised lung, or to the brain, and cause a stroke.

For periods of time I manage to calm down. My monitor numbers change very little. Every few minutes the monitor sounds an alarm. It can go on and on. No one rushes in because it is likely a monitor problem, not a patient problem.

At times my breathing eases. I spend long periods doing nothing but waiting. I try to read. I watch what goes on around me.

I see a fair amount of schmoozing. A policeman sits at a nurse's computer for more than a half-hour, leaning back in the desk chair, talking animatedly to someone out of my line of sight.

Doctors, nurses, and nursing assistants come by from time to time. Some listen to my lungs and heart. (*Take a deep breath. Again. Again. Now breathe normally.*) Most ask when I started having symptoms. I confess there were signals I ignored three days ago: unusual shortness of breath with very little exertion and gaining five pounds overnight, a sign of unusual fluid retention. These I knew were signals of heart problems. I denied them. I told myself I was still recovering from hiatal hernia surgery three weeks earlier. I should have known better. The signs were there Wednesday. Today is Saturday.

I never realized I had an arrhythmia, an irregular heartbeat. I knew I had a high pulse, because I used a pulse oximeter to check absorption. I did not feel my rapid pulse. I definitely felt my shortness of breath. As an asthmatic with COPD and missing a section of my right lung after cancer surgery, I am familiar with shortness of breath. This was more severe.

After hours in the ER I am rolled to an elevator, down some halls, and into the ICU. Kelly, my ICU nurse, tells me I am "confined to bed." She shows me how to operate the bed, raising and lowering the head and the area under my knees. My hospital gown is tangled with two IV lines and the monitor wires attached to various parts of my chest. Kelly untangles it. She offers me a fresh gown or, if I prefer, I can wear nothing but a sheet. The sheet is enough.

The way to feel better is to sit—not lie down—quietly. Lying down makes it worse.

Kelly has a soothing effect as she asks about my medical history and medications in an unhurried voice. I feel tension melt away. A tech comes in to draw blood, the first of many who will do this around the clock.

A pulmonary therapist brings my first breathing treatment. These treatments are familiar. They help. I will get them every four hours but can ask for them more frequently.

I spend the first night sitting up. I drowse but don't really sleep. The monitor keeps track of my vitals. My IVs drip. Alarms sound, and the nurse or the nursing assistant comes in to push buttons to shut the alarms up or check if the monitor wires are properly attached to my chest. I can see the monitor's display. My oxygen absorption is staying up. My blood pressure is in a desirable range. My pulse is high. I will this number to change.

The hospital physician asks me if I have any pain.

"A headache and a backache," I say.

"If we give you morphine for pain, it may also help your breathing."

I am injected with morphine. My breathing eases. I almost feel normal. My heart still races. I sleep, wake, sleep, wake. I have additional sedation for some of my procedures, which I barely remember. I suspect the morphine and the sedatives keep big feelings of anxiety at bay. Patricia doesn't have these to help her. She is worried.

The first doctor who comes to see me Sunday morning is the surgeon who operated on my hiatal hernia three weeks ago. I'm not sure I could list all the doctors who check on me. In addition to the surgeon who repaired my hernia, I am visited by my pulmonologist, another hospital pulmonologist, at least three "hospital physicians," an emergency room physician, my kidney doctor, a cardiologist (my own cardiologist does not practice in this hospital), a physician's assistant in cardiology, and a physician's assistant in urology (because I have had blood in my urine.) He urges me to see the urologist for whom he works when I am released. I suspect he is trying to drum up business. I ask a couple of my other doctors if I need to see a urologist. They say there is no need.

More than a dozen nurses and another dozen nursing assistants see me during my stay. Numerous phlebotomists draw blood, respiratory therapists give me treatments, and even a therapy dog comes to cheer me up. I have a huge team devoted (although somehow "devoted" doesn't feel like quite the right word) to my care. Who is in charge? Who heads the team? Can it really be considered a team? Who reconciles differing opinions if any come up? In a big way it is up to me, but I am on morphine, not quite all there. I tend to consider my pulmonologist being in charge. I'm not sure she sees it that way.

All my prescriptions are signed by one of the hospital physicians who visited me briefly three times during my stay. *Take a deep breath. Again. Again. Now breathe normally.* A lot of the communications among the various parties take place in my computerized chart, which I don't get to see. Some doctors explain the treatment and options. One conversation about the pros and cons of a particular medication takes place in my presence between two doctors, as if I am not there. The doctors reach a decision to prescribe it. Then one of them explains their reasoning. I ask questions. I get answers.

Procedures requiring me to fast (including drinking nothing) are postponed twenty-four hours, so I must fast again the next day. Nurse's aides come in during the night and put the water pitcher near me and urge me to drink. I have to remind them that I am not supposed to eat or drink anything and ask them to put the pitcher out of my reach, in case I forget.

Jonah, my son, comes to visit me from Oklahoma. He is good company, but I am not sure I am. I doze off a lot. He brought his laptop and is able to use the hospital Wi-Fi to connect to his university and work remotely. He uses his computer to go online and investigate the diagnoses and medications prescribed. His questions sometimes surprise the doctors. From my perspective, he is an important part of the medical team.

My career has involved paying close attention to processes and helping people figure out the opportunities to improve them. I can't help but pay attention to the hospital process. Much of it is good. For the most part the nurses, nursing assistants, and respiratory therapists are excellent caregivers. Most of the staff members who draw my blood, in what seems like a dozen times a day and another dozen times a night, do a good job, but their processes are compartmentalized. They draw the prescribed blood and move to the next patient.

One respiratory therapist wears heavy perfume. I think she should know better than to wear a scent around a patient with respiratory problems. In an unhurried moment, I ask a nursing assistant if there is a policy on perfume and I tell her why. She says she will take care of it. I tell her I don't want to get the therapist in trouble. She tells me it will be no problem. There is a way to request a different therapist without explanation. My next therapist is scent-free.

After a week—four days in ICU and three in more general care—I am turned out of the hospital into the Valley of the Sun. Heart failure. Failure. Failure of the heart. I don't like what they call it very much. I will go into a rehab program to help me learn to "live with heart failure." Live with failure.

There will be lots of pills to take. Blood will be drawn weekly. I'll need other tests. My diet must seriously restrict salt. I need to closely monitor my weight and whether there are any signs of swelling in my ankles and feet.

I am not a failure. I am a lucky guy. I have a wife who loves me, worries about me, and insists that I take care of myself. My humongous medical team helped me pull through. I still wonder how the system is coordinated and bet that, like all systems, it can be improved. In the hospital, my heart's ejection fraction (the effectiveness with which it pumps blood) dropped to 30. With rehab and medications, it is now at 50. An ejection fraction of 55 to 60 is normal. I am clearly improved. I do not have complete heart failure. I really don't feel like a failure at all.

I am a lucky guy. My Medicare and supplementary insurance covered practically all of the costs. I imagine the stress of not having insurance in such a situation. Caring friends visited and called me. My wife's employer was more than kind about her missing work to be with me. My son was able to bring some of his work with him and help me in the hospital. My daughter came after him, the day after I was released, and helped me get back on my feet. I am supported by a lot of love.

I am a very lucky guy. ∾

You'll Never Forget Your First

Matt Estrada

It's the summer of 1982, and I've just been offered a job at our corner drugstore. My parents pay me for the chores I perform around the house, but this marks the first time I will earn money from a real job. As much as I like to convince myself that my chores are like a real job, they are nothing in comparison. Unlike my household chores I won't be allowed to take breaks whenever I want, and dragging my job responsibilities out for days at a time will not be acceptable to my boss. I will be punching a time clock, and all the luxuries of time that I've taken for granted for so long will fade. All the complaints I verbalize while performing my chores seem silly as I think of the expectations that go along with having a job.

Of course, without job experience, all my expectations come from my imagination. I begin a list of the pros and cons of having a job. After several hours of writing, I realize I only have a few reasons swaying me one way or the other. The pros include making my own money while gaining job experience that will help me join the workforce when I graduate high school. Another pro to having a job is that it will keep me busy during summer days that drag on longer than they should. The cons consist of not being able to enjoy time with my friends during the summer days that drag on longer than they should.

I laugh at the only con that came to mind when compiling the list. Enjoying summertime with my friends won't teach me things that future prospective employers will want to see. I didn't see any section on the job application asking whether I have experience having fun with my friends.

When I tell my friends about my new job they all react as though I tell them I'm considering taking drugs. Why would

I willingly give up my summer, they wonder. Not a single one of them is happy about my opportunity, and it makes me see for the first time how selfish my friends are. And I will now appear on the government grid; filing taxes is part of having a job, but a price can't be attached to what I will gain.

My first day of real employment arrives, and I feel pride as I prepare for the day. Now I have a purpose and can act like an adult, and for the first time the sensation of making my own way in this world consumes me. The feeling is different from the day I hit a game-winning homerun. I will never forget the feeling of rounding each base, knowing that when I stepped on home plate it would be the run that won the game. That homerun will always be a great memory, and no one can ever take that away from me. The feeling I have right now, as I prepare for my first day of work, is something different altogether.

After my shower I wipe the steam from the mirror. For the first time in my life I look at my reflection and I see someone new. Life in this small Arizona mining town has its own pros and cons. The great thing about life in a small town is that everyone knows you. The bad thing about life in a small town is that everyone knows you. I've seen my reflection countless times before, but this time it shows me the person I hope to be. For fifteen years of my life I woke up knowing exactly how each day would unfold. Now that I'm sixteen I have no idea what to expect, and it's a feeling I never want to lose.

Once the prepping for my new job is complete, I exit my room and see my mom sitting at the dining room table. My younger brother doesn't understand why I can't stay and play with him, and he sulks in his chair with his arms folded across his body as he fixes his gaze on the floor.

I must admit, I didn't expect the disappointment from my friends about my new-found employment. I thought everyone who mattered to me would be happy for me, but that's not the case. My little brother's anger is easy to understand, however. After all, we've been inseparable until now.

"Oh, look at my son going to his first day of his new job."

"Do I look okay, Mom?"

"You look wonderful," she says, brushing back my hair. "I'm so proud of you.

"Thanks, Mom."

The look in my mother's eyes shows me how happy she is for me. I know she's nervous to see her son off on his first day of employment, but she does her best to hide her fears. It must be difficult to see your children make the leap into adulthood. My mom's been through it before with my two older brothers when they left for college. I'm the first of her children to get a job while in high school, so I'm sure she isn't prepared for this turn of events. She probably thought she had two more years to prepare for my becoming an adult, and this path to adulthood that found me in a world of endless pathways must have thrown her for a loop.

"You look so grown up," she says as she wraps her arms around me. My mother's hugs are magical. They heal all types of ailments, from sore throats, fevers, and stomach aches to cuts and bruises. I always wondered why there was never a bottle of medicine labeled "Mom's Hugs" in the medicine aisle at drugstores. Even though I didn't need her healing hug in this situation, it felt magical just the same.

"I better get going," I say as she holds on to me a little longer.

"I know you have to go. You're going to do great."

Life is good for the next four weeks. Of course this is not Walgreen's or CVS or anything close to that. But my corner drug store with its handful of aisles and prescription drug offerings doesn't need to be more than what it is. My job is offering me an opportunity to learn something while planning for my future.

At the beginning of my fifth week of work, my boss wants to talk.

"Matthew, I need to speak with you in my office," my boss says to me when I enter the store.

"Yes, sir."

"Have a seat."

Sliding into the old lumpy chair stationed in front of his desk, a blanket of uncomfortable silence drapes itself around my shoulders. The silence contrasts the noises of business being conducted in the store beyond his office door, which is where I'd rather be at the moment. I'm not sure of the proper etiquette to use here, since I've never navigated these waters of my first job. Do I look at him, or do I continue to stare at his desk while he stares out the window? Memories of my encounter with a rattlesnake invade my mind. Fighting the urge to move was the toughest part of that encounter, and I find myself trying to avoid alarming my boss with any sudden movement.

My boss' office serves as an example of organized chaos. Everything appears out of place, with no organization to it whatsoever. Stacks of paper litter the entire room, with paper strewn about the floor. His calendar displays the month of July while we are currently in October. Notes he writes to himself are tacked on every wall.

He begins to fidget, rubbing his neck before wringing his hands. He shuffles papers as sweat stains appear on his shirt. He opens and closes every drawer on his desk, sitting back in his chair as if he is upset about not finding what he was looking for. He leans forward, placing his elbows on his desk as he cups his face with his hands. Sweeping his hair back with his hands, he rocks back and forth in his chair, causing a "nails-across-the-chalkboard" sound.

"Matthew, do you enjoy—"

I lean closer to his desk, eager to hear any spoken words.

"Do you enjoy working here?" He doesn't look at me when he asks the question.

"Yes, I enjoy working here very much."

"Why do you enjoy it? I mean, what is it about this job you enjoy so much?" He finally looks me in the eyes but then turns his gaze to the wall behind me.

"It makes me feel good to know I'm being productive while I'm learning new things. I mean, this is my first job, so there's nothing to compare it to, but it's very enjoyable."

He lowers his head towards his desk while loosening the top button on his shirt. He rubs his neck as he mumbles something under his breath. I've witnessed the delivery of different types of bad news before, and his delivery reminds me of getting the news about a death in the family.

"Have I done something wrong?"

"Not at all, and that's what makes this so difficult." He wraps his hands around his coffee cup, though it holds no coffee.

"I don't understand."

"I have to let you go."

"Let me go? What do you mean?"

"I have to fire you!" he shouts; then he places his hands over his mouth as if he just blurted out a profanity in church. This is far from easy for my boss. Watching how difficult this is for him indicates this may be the first time he's ever fired anyone.

"Help me understand what I've done wrong."

"This has nothing to do with your job performance."

"Then what is it?"

"I've been friends with your father since we were kids, and he's asked me to fire you."

"Why does my father want you to fire me?"

"Your father is a proud man, but he fears with you working here people in town will think he can't support his family."

"My father has a great job; he makes more than enough money to support us."

"Yes, but he feels the people in town are beginning to think otherwise."

"I don't know what to say. I'm sorry you were put in this position to fire me."

"You're a great kid, and you've been a great employee. Maybe he'll change his mind down the road."

At sixteen years old, I didn't know that being fired from my first job was just one obstacle in a life filled with obstacles to overcome. Life did go on, and I have faced different types of rejection—in love, friendship, family, and other jobs. But I know I'll never forget my first time of getting rejected. ~

Desert Oasis

Colleen Grady

It sounded like a good idea. "Let's live where people vacation, and vacation where other people work." That's the spin Terry pitched to me. After many years together, he tapped into my favorite things: travel, vacations, and sun. Exchanging the moist, gray days of Seattle for the promise of a dry, sunny place tempted me.

There was just one glitch. I didn't want to move.

I wasn't unhappy living in Washington state. My roots, friends, and family lived in Seattle. Growing up as an only child, I longed for older siblings. Cousins were my first friends. I treasured my long-term girlfriends. I met some of them in my Bluebirds group in the fifth grade, and we were still close. My heart belonged to the Pacific Northwest—although the area wasn't perfect.

Washington weather was notorious. I was tired of the smell of wet wool in the winter and wearing long-sleeved turtlenecks in June. Continuous weeks of rain produced slippery green slime on patios and decks. One Memorial Day on a camping trip in Eastern Washington, it poured so hard I could have used a wet suit inside the tent. I spent many Fourth of Julys indoors in Seattle because it was so wet outside. Who wanted to roast s'mores under an umbrella?

Every winter I plotted how to swing a warm weather getaway and escape the drizzly days. Sleuthing out cheap airfares and scoring the best reasonable accommodations became more than a hobby: it was a priority. Catching the sun produced rewards. Soaking up the rays while slathered with coconut lime lotion made me feel whole and a lot thinner. I'm not a string bean, and I knew brown fat looked better than white fat any day.

Let's face it: sun bathing is much easier than dieting. Plus, upon returning home from a winter vacation, a golden tan guaranteed envious looks from friends and foes.

Terry asked me if I would like to move to Arizona. I took it as a rhetorical question. With a shrug, I concurred, "Sure." During our many years together, pipedreams appeared and then quickly disappeared. Previously he'd proposed moving to Belize, Palau, and the Marshall Islands, none of which he had ever visited. Those exotic moves never developed beyond a smattering of e-mails and calls to realtors and travel agencies. I had no reason to believe his inclination to relocate us to the Southwest would produce any different results.

But it proved to be different. Even the persistent calls from an eager realtor in Phoenix regarding business opportunities didn't set off any alarms for me. There had been others before him. I felt sorry for the realtor; he was wasting his time. Little did I know the realtor was hatching a business deal called Desert Oasis.

Terry, 49, an established and self-employed Seattle attorney, was fed up with practicing law. He wasn't a shark, and he hated the deadlines and the lying clients. His mid-life crisis was ripe. Always an idea guy, he dreamed plenty. He wanted to reinvent himself. Fortunately for me he didn't gravitate towards the classic red-Corvette-with-a-foxy-young-blonde-in-the-passenger-seat scenario.

My mid-life crisis was resolved thanks to Terry's encouragement. At 48 I returned to the original college I attended, Western Washington University. In 1969, after three years of wasted tuition, I had skipped off campus to be a stewardess for Alaska Airlines. I was certain I would never look back. Wrong. I spent the next thirty years uncomfortable while skirting all conversations discussing college degrees.

Lots of middle-agers like me return to school to finish a degree. I moved to Bellingham and into a single room in a dorm. What an opportunity to reconcile the past with the present! Sitting in the same cafeteria I frequented in the '60s, I marveled

Colleen Grady

again at the views of the Bay and the Olympic Mountains. The vintage plastic molded chairs had held up well.

I loved the entire experience. Not many relationships sanction a year apart to fix old mistakes. I owed Terry.

In April of 1996 we boarded a plane in Seattle for the flight to Phoenix. If a deal was struck for Desert Oasis, relocation was inevitable. As the flight attendant rattled through the safety instructions, I told myself change is good. Nothing is forever. What was the worst thing that could happen? My vision included resort-style living, palm trees, the scent of orange blossoms, a lagoon-shaped pool, and sunset patio parties sharing margaritas with new friends. Surely, with the name Desert Oasis, it promised all that.

We walked out of Sky Harbor airport into 89-degree weather. We stepped up for a luxury rental car with a white diamond finish. Terry drove. I fooled with the car radio, opted for a happy station, and cranked it up. The sounds of mariachis bounced around the car as we rolled onto Highway 10. Terry guaranteed a scenic ride.

Grand Avenue cuts diagonally across the West Valley. We easily maneuvered onto it. Cruising by Sun City, we noticed strip mall parking lots overflowing with cars displaying out-of-state license plates. Snowbirds, no doubt.

We followed Grand Avenue as it merged into US Route 60. Cacti on the desert floor replaced communities and commercial buildings. As we whizzed along, an occasional palo verde or mesquite tree dotted the rural landscape. Glancing at Terry, I realized his enthusiasm increased proportionately to the decrease in housing and stores. Hmm; troubling for a city girl.

We travelled past random humble houses as ramshackle store fronts popped up along the south side of the now two-lane road. Long-haul trucks dominated the highway in both directions, leaving contrails of dust on our windshield. Faded "For Sale" signs dangled off leaning fences in front of vacant properties. A railroad track and nothing else ran parallel to the north side of US Route 60.

How much longer? It was called an oasis. There had to be more than sunshine and saguaros.

My understanding was that Desert Oasis stood alone in the Sonoran Desert. The realtor's map placed it just before Morristown. Morristown had less than 200 residents. It would be sixteen years later that its only claim to fame would be Grumpy Cat, the Internet sensation. But we stopped before Morristown.

Out of nowhere I spied a tall pole with the sign "Desert Oasis RV and Mobile Home Park. A full service park." Pulling off the highway, we parked adjacent to a wide grassy strip. Two gas pumps had signs: $1.35 per gallon. An A-frame building appeared to be freshly but thickly painted red, white, and blue. The signage stated "Store and Office." Two Budweiser promotional banners hung across the store front. I checked my makeup in the passenger mirror. We got out of the car and opened the door.

Terry dashed inside looking for the sellers. After pushing through a thick wall of second-hand smoke, I stopped to get my bearings. Smelly. Sticky. Eeew. A lousy first impression.

Squinting with stinging eyes, I tried to take in the scene. Next to me a middle-aged guy muttered, "Marlboro Reds." Without looking at the cashier, he slapped his money on the counter. A fluorescent light bounced off his big brass buckle. It had a buffalo on it.

Are there buffalos here?

My thoughts were interrupted by a screeching little girl demanding candy. Her mother, in a blue plaid Western shirt, ignored her daughter and searched the canned food shelf. She settled on Spaghetti O's. The only other sounds came from thirteen-year-old LeAnn Rimes on a radio and the whirling blades from a floor fan. I told myself that the store had a kitschy Western-Americana funky kind of vibe that could be fun—with a few changes.

• Note to self: Buy No Smoking signs ASAP.

I found Terry at a blue picnic table inside. The sellers— Margaret, the mother, and Pauline, the daughter—positioned themselves next to each other facing out, able to see most of the store. They sat like a pair of guard dogs. The daughter, seeing me approach, rolled her eyes as if to say, "Get a load of this one."

It was an odd place to talk about finances and business. The mother-daughter duo, both smoking, were mirror images of each other. Large women. Each wearing a peasant-style muumuu and a judgmental expression, kind of a cross between a sneer and a weird grin.

Terry introduced me. They didn't appear interested. I babbled some "Isn't this exciting"-type comments that fell totally flat. I sat down and shut up. Obviously my expectation for a cheery meet-and-greet was completely unrealistic. The women spoke exclusively to Terry. I was invisible to them. He was animated and eating it up. Me, not so much.

The women laid out the perils of owning and operating Desert Oasis, a former KOA campground with a cute motel-sized swimming pool. I learned there were ninety-three hook-up pads for temporary and permanent residents. I knew I would never be either. The compound consisted of the gas pumps, a propane station, a Laundromat, a paneled rec room with a pool table, public bathrooms and showers, and, of course, the general store. This was a bigger deal than I originally thought.

Margaret, in her sixties, was an aggressive woman with a no-nonsense attitude. She presented a hardline policy of dealing with the park residents, employees, and customers and emphasized that the people were the greatest threat and hazard for Desert Oasis. Somewhat intimidated, I decided to get my Irish up and probe a bit.

"I'd like to know about some of the people who have lived here the longest."

"They're all the same. You can't trust any of 'em. They'll rob ya blind. Don't believe a word they say. We've got rules and fines here. You gotta watch 'em every minute."

And apparently she did.

I had a new motto for their "full service" park: We're not satisfied until you're *not* satisfied.

I didn't give up. "Do you have regular customers in the store? Are there special requests?"

"Don't even think about being friends with any of them," Margaret said. "They're losers. They'll buy whatever you've got, if they don't steal it first. This goes for the employees too."

I didn't need to look for the "Customer is Always Right" sign in this store.

Wow, I thought. *Without the residents, employees and customers, what was left?*

I would soon find out.

The mother-daughter team suggested some peculiar items we would need to buy and to keep in mind. Urinal cakes, swamp cooler pads, monsoons, $3 showers, dust devils, valley fever, stick houses, haboobs (Arizona dust storms,) meth cooks, and javelinas (wild boars in the Arizona desert.) It was a foreign language. What were we doing? Terry, attentive and ever smiling, was unwavering. He hated practicing law and couldn't wait to do something physical and with his hands. He wanted in; they wanted out.

I was beyond conflicted. This was unlike any desert oasis I imagined. How supportive could I be? How selfish was I?

My greatest fear tormented me. I had to ask even though I knew the answer.

"Do you see snakes in the park?"

Pauline gloated. "Hell, yes. What do ya think? They live here. Matter of fact, there were two rattlers swimmin' in the pool last night."

Right then I knew I would never swim in that cute pool.

Surprisingly, Margaret caught my grimace; she added that Bill could help me with snakes.

Help me with snakes?

"He got one last week off the Johnsons' porch. It was wrapped around a bicycle tire real tight. Bill took his time and was glad to get him. "

I hated it but managed to spit out, "Good to know. Now tell me some more about Bill."

"He thinks he's a mountain man. Works part-time in the store and part-time outside. "

"But what about Bill and the snakes?"

"Oh, that. He hunts mostly diamondbacks. Puts 'em in gunny sacks."

"And does what with them?"

"Makes hat bands out of them. Real pretty. He'll probably try to sell ya one."

"Uh, you know, I'm not really a big hat person." Why did I even wear this linen suit?

• Note to self: Never, ever go to Bill's or open a gunny sack.

Margaret and Terry were talking numbers and terms and conditions. I flashed back to when Terry predicted I would relish Desert Oasis and the local characters. I loved quirky people and savored crazy stories. Desperately hoping to tap into some of that, I asked Pauline about the woman in the front.

"That's Sally Jo. She's a real troublemaker, stirs things up. Watch out for her."

"How long has she worked here?"

"About five years. She's lived here longer, though."

Sally Jo had toned arms in a tight tank top, Daisy Dukes that looked good on her, and gray suede ankle boots. Yet another smoker, she had one hanging out of the corner of her mouth. Another forgotten cigarette, with a long ash growing, balanced off the edge of a metal ashtray. It sat next to the cash register.

Sally Jo hoisted a heavy case of something up onto the counter. Her face, wrinkled and weathered, revealed a senior age. Her body did not.

I learned she was a widow. Her husband had worked highway construction. They had traveled with their children to wherever the jobs were. They were happy. His last job was on U.S. Route 60. He died of a heart attack practically in front of the store.

Sally Jo didn't want to leave the last place they stayed. She raised her three boys by herself in a fifth-wheel travel trailer. Her youngest son still lived with her, along with his teenage girlfriend and their baby. They all shared the same travel trailer in Desert Oasis.

I smiled at Sally Jo. She half-smiled back at me with sad, brown eyes. I got up from the table and walked over to her. She was pricing and stocking cans of chili.

"You must be Sally Jo. I wanted to meet you. My name is Colleen."

"Nice to meet you, ma'am."

"Oh, please, it's Colleen."

"Um, are you guys gonna buy the park?"

"Probably. But while watching you buzz around, I see there's lots I'd need to learn."

"Um…would you…keep some employees?"

"Definitely."

"Count me in! I can show you everything. Introduce you to everyone. Nice folks live here. We watch out for each other. Like family. Just yesterday, Louise Brown heard Johnny Miller got laid off—again. She felt bad. Started frying up a bunch of chicken for him. That's our Louise."

For the first time since we arrived, I sensed there was goodness at Desert Oasis.

• Note to self: Disregard all previous advice, and proceed with kindness.

I did. ∿

Making Friends in Arizona

Dawn Gunn

The car air conditioner whined all the way to Arizona in that August of 1972. Summer in the Southwest didn't feel like it did in Illinois. The Southwest was dry, hot, and physically draining. Lightning illuminated the sky, and dust blew everywhere. I wanted to go home, but I was also excited about our new house and our new life. Mom and Dad said I had a big room, and I would be very happy there. I could start kindergarten in September just days before my fifth birthday.

Our new life got its start in Glendale, Arizona, a newer city back then. The large tri-level house included a big balcony in my parents' room where my brothers and I could sit. Dad painted a desert mural on the wall in the living room. He put saguaros, ocotillo, and a lot of desert life in that painting. It made me fall in love with the desert and made the move a little easier. I missed my home and family back in Illinois.

School started in September, but I don't think my teacher liked me. Maybe I should have recognized this as the first sign of my new life in the Southwest. It would be a challenging one.

My teacher, Mrs. Cacoon, seemed frustrated that I already knew my alphabet and that I could read and write before I even started kindergarten. I had three brothers a decade older than myself. Of course I could read and write. They made me learn. They said I would be a dummy if I didn't know how, so I learned and I liked it. Reading and writing would serve as my escape as my existence became more difficult with my new life in the desert.

Not long after I started kindergarten my mom got sick and needed surgery. It took a long time for her to recover, and during her recovery my maternal grandmother came to stay at our

102

house and take care of us. Grandma wasn't the most loving person in the world. My grandmother's stern, aggressive behavior made her presence difficult for my parents. It felt like it took forever, but my mom finally got better and life was good again.

Shortly after my mom's recovery something went wrong with Dad's architecture business, and Mom and Dad said we had to move again. We soon moved to a new house in Phoenix. It wasn't too far from our old house, but it was much smaller. The boys all had to share a room. I still had a room to myself, but it felt smaller than my Glendale room.

The house sounded noisier, probably due to the smaller size, but we did have a pool with a diving board and a nice patio. I liked it, but I still missed the one in Glendale. We didn't get to live there long enough and too much happened in such a short time—a new life, two new houses, two new schools. I felt so confused.

Little did I know that we would only enjoy one happy year in that second house. My dad got sick and stopped working. He went to the hospital frequently and looked tired all the time, and he couldn't play with me anymore either. He went to the VA Hospital for the last time after Christmas in 1973, suffering from congestive heart failure. On January 27, 1974, my dad died, leaving us alone.

A well-meaning person made a mistake and told me my dad "went to sleep forever." Long after his funeral I waited for my father to wake up. In the difficult weeks, months, and years that followed, I kept hoping he would rise and rescue me.

We had nothing—no money, no insurance. Mom couldn't even drive. My oldest brother, David, took on the role of the man of the house. He drove my mom to work, took me to school, and made sure we all had what we needed each day. He even tried to help with money and grocery shopping. He did this from January to August 1974, when my mom married another man only eight months after the death of my dad. She married a commanding, castigating military man who could afford to provide a comfortable life for her and her kids. We moved once again. Another new house, another new school, and a new "daddy."

David left in September to join the United States Air Force. We saw him occasionally for short visits. He didn't come back to stay in Arizona until decades later when he prepared to retire and received his last set of orders for Luke Air Force Base in Litchfield, Arizona, outside of Phoenix.

During David's absence, my relationship with my step-father was a caustic one. We fought constantly, and many times it would end with him becoming violent. My mom called David for advice, but nothing ever came of it. We continued to fight often, and my step-father continued to go too far. More than once I had to cover up the evidence left on my body.

The Lord had taken my first daddy. I often wondered when he would take the other one. I prayed so hard for it. For eleven years I waited for the opportunity to walk out and leave that life. I never imagined having anything less than bitterness and anger toward that man, until I married and started a family of my own.

When I was pregnant with my first child, Chantelle, my step-dad made the first move to develop a meaningful relationship with me. He came by my apartment every morning before work just to talk over a cup of coffee. I found this to be strange and out of character for him, but I was open to changing the dynamics of our relationship.

I wanted my daughter to have grandparents. My mom and I were close all my life. Having a good relationship with my step-dad would make spending time with her easier. My mom loved her husband as much as she loved me. Sometimes I think she felt caught in the middle of everything and just didn't know what to do with the situation. She hated to see me hurt, but she feared losing my step-dad if she pushed back too hard. Now I would be able to have a relationship with both of them, and my daughter would have the grandparents she deserved.

My step-dad and my mom bought everything I needed in order for me to be as ready as possible for my baby to enter the world. After Chantelle was born we started going on family trips together, and one night my step-dad made a profound statement. He said, "My granddaughter is beautiful. History doesn't have to repeat itself, Dawn."

After catching my breath, I emotionally explained, "I have no intention of repeating history, Dad. When I get angry I'll walk away or lock her in her room until *I'm* calm." I know I saw tears in his eyes; to this day he swears it was allergies.

I don't know what prompted the change, but I think my step-dad finally realized the importance of family. Perhaps the years of fervent praying for him finally paid off. I imagine my mom also prayed for him. Perhaps the Lord just finally softened his heart or opened his eyes to what could be if he would just let it. It didn't matter; my only focus was how nice it would be to have my daughter loved and cared for by both her grandparents.

My husband and I have had three more children since then. The youngest is named after my step-father and has proudly nicknamed himself "Forrest 2." My step-dad is 82 now, and when he leaves this world to join our Lord Jesus I will lose the only dad I've ever known until we meet again just as the Lord has promised.

I came to Arizona forty-two years ago. Many challenges took me to my limits, but I don't regret a single one of them. Their chemistry has formed the matrix of who I am today, and I like me. I wake up every morning as my own friend, supporter, and cheerleader.

I use my story to help others find peace in themselves and their stories. I share my experiences with those who struggle with dealing with the past. I provide support and guidance for friends and family who have dreams and goals but are too frightened to attempt them. I council those who feel afraid to love themselves because someone told them, through words or actions, that they have no worth. I use my story to help others realize the truth about themselves: life is to be cherished and lived to the fullest. Forgiving and loving yourself and the Lord is key.

My mom is gone now, and the man she married eight months after my dad died—the man who was, for many years, my enemy—is now my best friend. ❧

Rethinking Life's Truths

(Restoring the Turkey Pecking Order)

Donna Hamill

The turkey hens stand face to face, beak to beak. They look like they are kissing, but they are not.

Each one puffs out her feathers to look larger and intimidate the opponent. One hen opens her mouth; that's a mistake, because the other one shoves her closed beak inside it and then pushes her backwards hard, like a bull dog.

The open-mouthed hen is taken by surprise and has no choice but to back up—back, back, ending up in the gangly branches of a creosote bush. Still, the hen asserting her dominance does not let go.

I scold myself, because I should have known what would happen to the pecking order when I returned one of the turkeys to the fenced run.

She hatched a brood of babies about six weeks ago. The free-range run has chain-link fencing with openings large enough for young ones to walk through. So I separated the family into a smaller 10' x 10' enclosure with half-inch chicken wire all around. There, Mother Hen kept the babies warm and safe while they grew and became strong. It's time now for Mother to return to the larger run with the other adults, while the poults must remain in their brooder pen for a while until they grow too large to fit through the chain-link openings.

I contemplate stopping the battle but quickly dismiss the idea. This is their way of asserting dominance, and perhaps I have no right to interfere.

Inside the enclosure the turkeys have developed a complex social hierarchy, or pecking order, in which each individual has an established place. It's like a list ranked from high to low.

There is a dominant male (tom or gobbler) who is naturally on top of the power structure. There is also a dominant female who assumes more or less power depending upon the presence of a tom. Then the list progresses downward to the lowest rungs in the social order, often ending with the young who cannot yet stand their ground.

People sometimes borrow the term "pecking order" to describe the stratification or leadership roles in society. The rights and privileges associated with a CEO, for example, are different than those of a clerk.

As for the turkeys, their behavior is governed by natural laws developed, honed, and practiced generation after generation. It is the way nature intended them to be, and I respect it.

The struggle is also unavoidable. I might as well let this thing play out while I can watch to ensure they don't get too intense. I grab a nearby lawn chair and drag it to a shady spot underneath a mesquite tree.

It's early in the morning, and the Arizona sun is still low in the eastern sky. Brilliant oranges, yellows, and reds streak the azure blue horizon. However, this is only a small preview of the awe-inspiring show that will occur this evening during the world-famous Arizona sunset.

The brightness stings my eyes so I tilt my wide-brimmed garden hat, pulling it down on the right-hand side to block out the glowing ball. I can't see the turkey feather slipped into my hat band but I know it's there, dancing in the light morning breeze.

This is the first time I've owned turkeys, but I've raised chickens all my life. Some chicken breeds are mild mannered while others have real attitude.

So far my Narragansett turkeys have not been particularly aggressive. This is, in fact, the first time I've witnessed forceful behavior at all. I suppose their mellow nature has lulled me into forgetting about the group dynamics that go on inside every poultry pen.

As a human being I sometimes forget about the importance of their world. For example, when I add or remove poultry the hierarchies shift. In this case there was a dominant female already established in the run when I add the mother hen. The social order is now in upheaval. Dominance must be established.

The hens are not trying to be cruel to each other. They are simply trying to establish the identity of the lead female.

I'm reminded of a fairy tale I read once to the children about an entire village of mice that could talk and act like humans. They had little town meetings and made plans about all kinds of important things. Giving human attributes to animals is called "personification," and it is only make believe.

Yet sometimes I think life in the chicken coop or turkey run is a lot like the mouse village. Everyone has his or her own status in society, and decisions are made about all sorts of group activities. They know the laws and culture, and everything works together for the common good. It's when humans get involved that things get turned topsy-turvy.

The open-mouthed hen is still stuck in the creosote bush and can be pushed backward no more. She twists and turns her beak this way and that trying to dislodge the other. Somehow she throws the aggressor off, escaping both the entangling limbs and the onslaught.

Now in the open ground again, she closes her beak and tries to regain her wits. I am surprised when she returns the attack by rushing the dominant female. Perhaps she will win the battle and assume the coveted role. I doubt it, as she is still weakened from her recent maternal duties.

Beak to beak again. Their two heads poised together, along with their long curved necks meeting at the breast, give the impression of a heart shape with each hen's beak, head, and neck forming one side.

They push and shove each other for a while, each gaining and losing ground. At several points they actually entwine their necks around each other, looking like two burly branches twisted together. I wonder how they can do that.

Then the dominant female uses her strong, sharp beak to grab the other hen's soft, red wattle hanging from her neck.

This seems like a particularly sensitive area, and the aggressor bites, pulls, and twists it mercilessly. This is when I stand up, ready to intervene. "That's gotta hurt," I whisper. However, there is no blood, and the tissue of the wattle is still intact. So I sit down again. They continue to take turns biting at each other's wattles, but no real damage is done.

Then the mother hen, who obviously has not learned from her first mistake, errs again. She opens her beak.

Instantly, the other hen seizes her chance. She jabs her closed beak into the open mouth and pushes the mother hen backward away from where I am sitting. First, the mother hen is backed into a green palo verde tree. Then she is thrust backwards again into the rear chain-link fence. That's as far as they can go.

The impact of hitting the fence knocks them both off balance. The mother hen closes her beak and shakes her head.

That's it. Mother Hen has had enough. She unpuffs her feathers and retreats. She runs like mad all the way to the water trough, which is near my chair.

The dominant female follows at a slow and confident stroll. When she arrives, the mother hen is quietly drinking. At this point I brace myself for another assault.

Evidently, however, unpuffing feathers must be similar to waving a white flag, because both hens are now drinking water together peacefully.

The dominant female has affirmed her position, and the social order has been restored. No one has been really hurt. Nothing more needs to be said.

I think there is a lesson to be learned here, some moral about the meaning of life. I file it in the back of my brain to think about later.

Our little self-sustainable farm has made me rethink many of life's truths. Caring for animals, growing vegetables, and being connected to the land is just so real and honest and good.

Trying to do these things in a hot, dry climate like Arizona has been challenging, though. For example, my husband and I were looking for a small self-sustaining flock of turkeys to provide meat for the table but were not sure the Narragansett breed could withstand the harsh environment. Fortunately, the turkeys are not only growing and physically thriving, they also seem very happy here. My husband and I are getting so much more from them than ever expected. Caring for them has been both enjoyable and fulfilling. As it turns out, they make us happy, too. ⚬∾

Sharing Sweat in Arizona

(A Legacy of Knowledge)

Donna Hamill

I want it known that I'm a grandma. That said, let me take stock of the situation.

A pale-colored mud covers my gloves and clothes. I'm kneeling on the ground, bent over a small trench, trying to repair a leak in my daughter and son-in-law's drip irrigation system.

The blood rushes to my head as I work in this upside-down position. Yet my wide-brimmed garden hat, its crown pressed tightly to my head, doesn't even threaten to fall off. The Narragansett turkey feather slipped into the band dances in the breeze, suggesting to the neighbors a lifestyle quite different from their own here in this housing tract.

Most people would hire someone to do this sort of work. It's not just the depressed economy that makes me so interested in saving a dollar, though that contributes to my commitment. Through the years I've accumulated a good number of useful skills. I'm trying to pass these on to my grown children. It is my way of empowering the next generation—leaving a legacy of knowledge.

The sun is in my eyes, and it's hot. The local weather report predicts 112 degrees today. Even at 7:30 A.M. it's already uncomfortable. I was here at dawn, because I knew there was hard work to do before the worst of the heat set in.

In Arizona there's no avoiding the heat. Being an avid heirloom vegetable gardener I've become accustomed to working outside in spite of it, doing chores in the early morning. My muscles are strong, and my body is acclimated to the environment—as much as is possible, anyway.

"Lots and lots of water," I remind myself as I take another gulp.

An old, stained, white woven-cotton dish towel is tied around my neck as a bandana. It's ugly but is a direct order from my dermatologist who says I have sensitive skin. It seems my Celtic ancestry has ill prepared me for life under the bright Southwest sun.

With my handheld garden spade, I take another scoopful of mud out of the hole and flick it aside. The wet mess goes splat on the ground. This isn't normal mud, because it acts like wet concrete. When it dries it will become hard as rock. Calcium carbonate forms a cement-like bond in this type of soil, which is called "caliche."

Having been born and raised in Arizona, I've heard the word. I just thought it meant "hard dirt" and didn't comprehend the depth of the problem. You see, I'd never actually seen caliche before.

At my own home nearby, the soil is sandy. When a shovel is pushed into the ground, sharp, abrasive, granules scratch and crunch along the metal spade as it slips unhindered downward to its full depth. My husband and I have easily hand-dug the trenches serving an otherwise-parched acreage with water. He taught me how to run water lines. Having more time during the day to practice this skill, I soon became the family expert.

Consequently, my past experiences all being with sand, I was surprised when I came to help my daughter start a garden in the backyard of her new home. It was our introduction to caliche.

Forget the shovel. It was useless. For a while we tried digging the backyard irrigation trenches using a large chisel and sledgehammer. Chisel a hole and then chisel sideways to flip up the sediment in layers. Chisel, flip, chisel, flip.

To plant a couple of small trees they borrowed a large impact hammer. I was not present and cannot describe this in detail. I'm sure it wasn't fun (although my daughter has corrected me saying, "It was a blast!")

My husband bought a load of construction block for the only logical solution for the garden—raised beds about two feet tall. He built two and she filled them with store-bought garden soil, adding bits of newspaper, straw, and kitchen scraps. It makes me smile, because she has done more with those raised beds than I have with my larger acreage. She is a good gardener.

"I found the leak!" I exclaim.

It's about time! Today I brought extra help—my other daughter and her boyfriend. We have been taking turns using the claw end of a heavy hammer to dig the caliche where the water is surfacing. It has taken an hour-and-a-half just to dig the stupid hole, which is no more than 10 inches deep.

Everyone positions themselves to view the problem.

"A pipe is leaking somewhere under the two-car driveway and seeping to this point where the concrete ends," I explain.

"That doesn't sound good," they echo together.

Then I add, "Something is not right here." The muddy water is blocking my view, and I attempt to clean out the hole for a better look.

I did not install the drip irrigation in their front yard. It existed when they purchased the house. I would not have used thin, flexible half-inch polyvinyl as a supply line underneath a concrete drive. My preference at home is to use more durable rigid materials everywhere, especially in sensitive areas such as under a driveway. Additionally, for a supply line I'd select a larger diameter pipe that would not restrict the flow.

Fortunately, however, the installers did slide the polyvinyl inside a larger 1.5" pipe acting as an outer conduit. With the mud cleaned out of the hole, we can all see the endpoint where the wider-diameter conduit stops and the soft polyvinyl emerges out of it and then continues its path to the water source.

"The inside line is leaking somewhere under the drive, and the outer tube is channeling water to this point," I explain.

Then my daughter says, "It wouldn't be leaking if Mom had installed it."

I smile at her vote of confidence but only momentarily as my mind is focused on the task at hand. I wipe the sweat off my forehead before it stings my eyes. Then I examine the situation.

"We've already located this one end of the line here where the water is accumulating. To repair it we must find the other end, where the pipe comes out on the other side of the concrete, and then replace the entire length underneath."

From the looks of their faces, I can see they feel overwhelmed. What makes the job worse, of course, is the unyielding caliche.

So, with some hesitation, we begin digging on the other side of the driveway hoping to find the other end of the pipe. While I'm standing near them watching their progress, a neighbor walks out of his house towards his car. He is openly staring at me with my wide-brimmed, turkey-feathered hat and my dingy white cotton bandana. I suppose I am not the typical landscape repairman.

"The neighbor can't believe my mother is repairing the drip system," my daughter explains.

"Maybe he wants my business card," I reply jokingly.

The temperature is rising quickly now, so we step up the pace.

I'm not quite sure why the conduit doesn't go straight across, but some digging reveals that it slants. This complicates our ability to locate the other end. Did the installers do that intentionally as a joke, I wonder.

Once the correct holes are dug in the rock-hard caliche, it's easy to make the repairs. In response to an earlier tip from my husband, I attach duct tape to the end of the damaged half-inch polyvinyl and then to a new double length of heavy-duty (SCH 40) three-quarter-inch pipe and pull it through inside the conduit from one side to the other. It works like a charm. (Thanks for the tip, honey!)

With the job finished, I collect my tools and kneel to put them into my hand-held tool box. One or two are covered with mud, so I wipe them off with the bottom of my t-shirt before putting them away.

"How's your computer running now?" my son-in-law asks as he bends over beside me.

"Great, now that you've worked with it." I return his smile, because I know it makes him feel good to contribute this expertise.

All of us, in fact, enjoy sharing skills with family members that save them money or improve their lives. Each of us, in turn, has opportunities to help someone else. For example, my husband and I know that our family will be there whenever we need help on the property or in the garden.

However, it goes deeper than sharing sweat. I've watched my younger family learn skills from my husband and me that they then add to their own tool belt. Things like how to adjust a hot water heater, change a toilet bowl float, replace a belt on the car, mend a sock, sew curtains, oil a sewing machine, plant corn, save seeds, can tomatoes at home, or cook with a double boiler. Then sometimes knowledge passes from younger to older, as is often the case with new technology.

Passing knowledge from one generation to another is how our family members help each other. Pretty soon, my daughter and son-in-law will know how to repair the drip system without help.

In the meantime, I intend to put myself in the middle of a muddy trench whenever it is helpful, for as long as I am physically able—hopefully, until I am a great-grandma. ∞

The Telephone

Elizabeth Kral

I lived through my early childhood during World War II, 1941 to 1945, with my parents and my dad's parents. Our house had the only telephone in a mining settlement of twenty or so houses east of Flagstaff.

Grampa mined rock until 1939, the year I was born, when a mine accident claimed his left foot. Gramma cared for me while Mom's hands grew gnarly doing woman's work.

Dad would rather have served in the military but continued as the family's sole supporter throughout the war. He drove his old pickup truck to the mine office every morning. After work he hunted and trapped in the forest at the top of the hill. With the extra cash he earned selling meat and pelts he sometimes bought us gifts, like hand lotion for Mom and coloring books for me.

We lived in the first house at the intersection of our cinder road and the paved road into Flagstaff. Miners too old for military service waited beside the telephone pole on the corner for a truck to take them to work. The truck rumbled past telephone poles carrying the line farther east to the mine entrance.

However, telephone service did not extend onto our road until April 1942. That's when Dad convinced the phone company to install a phone in our home. He stressed how the war's life-and-death situations demanded instant communication, and he promised free use to everyone on our road.

Our neighbors admired the two-foot-high golden oak telephone adorning our kitchen wall. Its graceful cathedral arch crowned two half-cup metal bells that looked like breastplates. Below the bells a horn protruded to carry a speaker's voice. A metal hook on the left side held the earpiece. A twist of the crank on the right brought on an operator who said, "Number, please."

Above the phone Dad tacked a page from a government pamphlet urging all Americans to "conserve and recycle metal, paper, and rubber." Then he hammered a nail into the wall alongside the phone and dangled a pencil on a string from the nail. People simply wrote what they needed to remember on the wall.

The wall soon became a combination calendar, to-do list, and telephone book. Sometimes, if I pestered Gramma long enough, she would read some of the writing to me. I asked Gramma to teach me to read. She said, "Yer only four years old. Yer too young yet."

She pulled me away from the writing as though the wall had just caught fire. But, as usual, she continued talking. "Go to school when yer six 'n study fer six years; then you'll read and write good like me."

Although neighbors often sat at our kitchen table awaiting calls, only my parents or grandparents were allowed to answer the phone. Gramma explained to me, "What if'n the caller is wanna leave a message fer pick up? Of if'n they wanna message be delivered?"

Oh, how I wanted to talk on the telephone myself. On sunny days I sat under the grape arbor imitating how adults spoke on the phone.

Mom often took me walking with her to deliver messages. She told me the names of everyone who lived in each house we passed. When we saw a blue star in the front window, it meant someone who lived there was away in uniform. One neighbor had two blue stars in the front window, and another had three.

———◦◦◦———

I liked being with Mom and Gramma when they were doing their important work. One day I climbed up on a kitchen chair beside the counter to watch Gramma make the awful-tasting margarine we used instead of butter. She plopped the greasy white glob into Mom's large mixing bowl, and after she broke a plastic capsule as big as her thumb knuckle she dripped its orange goo over the white stuff.

Then she grabbed both my hands, plunged them into the mess, and said, "Squeeze this 'til it looks like butter." I got queasy, the way I had the first time I had turned over a big rock and saw worms squiggle as though gasping for air. Gramma started lecturing. "N'er stay in the kitchen alone if'n somebody's on the telephone. They talk'n family secrets. Thar secrets're our secrets. We n'er tell anybody . . ."

One afternoon in July 1944 while playing Kick the Can in the road with my friends, we noticed our neighbor replacing her single blue star with a gold one. The next day, while coloring at the kitchen table, I overheard that neighbor talking on the phone about someone dying because of a bomb. I ran outside and hid under the grape arbor because I was afraid.

But I wasn't afraid because I heard scary talk. I didn't understand the word "bomb," and as for death, people were always talking about somebody dying. I was afraid because I had disobeyed Gramma. If she knew I had stayed to finish my picture instead of leaving as soon as the woman started her conversation, she might hide my crayons or spank me.

———◦◦◦———

A little more than a month later, for my fifth birthday on Saturday, August 12, Dad took me with him to the general store. He handed me a dollar bill. "Betty, he said, "you're old enough to pick out your own birthday gift. Look around and find something for yourself."

In the toy section at the rear of the store, my eyes settled on a little black patent purse. The purse was thin and lightweight. Its shiny metal clasp turned to reveal the inside had no lining or inner pockets like Mom's purse. It didn't matter. The only important thing was the shiny finish. I put the strap over my shoulder and walked through the aisles, imitating how Mother reviewed the shelves for items she might purchase.

Dad approved my selection and took me to the cash register. I placed the purse on the glass countertop and handed my dollar to the white-haired man on the opposite side. He looked at my father who nodded his okay.

Dad caught me eyeing the penny candies in the case under the glass counter. He told me to pick out five pieces. I could count to five because I just turned five. I chose my favorites, three root beer barrels and two wax red lips.

"I'm proud of you for picking out your own birthday present," Dad said as he parked his truck in front of our house. He handed me the bag of canned peaches to carry inside. Then he grabbed the sacks of flour and rice, smiled at me, and said, "You are so grown up." I felt happy about Dad's compliment and that he had bought canned peaches. I loved canned peaches more than any other food.

The next morning, I found out just what "grown up" meant to Dad. Young children go in a potty, and grownups use the outhouse! In her matter-of-fact manner, Mom told me, "Your father said you are big enough to use the outhouse." I cried each time she took me there.

It stunk. Daddy long leg spiders pranced—to where? Other spiders lurked on intricate webs. Did they leave their webs to eat? Did the flying bugs ever rest? Were other creepy crawlies hiding in the hole, waiting for someone to sit down? Worst of all, I feared I might fall in.

After a couple of days, I quit crying but reverted to childish antics and tantrums that brought familiar reprimands. Content in this comfort zone, I pushed the limits of attention seeking a little more every day.

Finally, Gramma said, "I can't turn my back on you fer a minute." As soon as the words left her mouth, I reached up and flattened my palm on the golden oak phone case. She turned and warned, "You git yer hand off the phone." I reached up and planted my other hand on the phone.

Gramma flew across the kitchen with her wooden spoon shouting, "You know yer not allowed to touch the phone!" Lucky for me, the bowl of the spoon broke off the handle on her first whack. She told my mother. But I didn't care.

Before supper I overheard Mom whispering to Dad in the

living room, "There are better ways to raise children."

Dad replied a little louder, "Spare the rod and spoil the child."

Mom, never argumentative, uncharacteristically answered, "Your thinking is old-fashioned. Betty is afraid to be grown up. We need to let her do something that makes her happy to be older."

The next day, Mom surprised me with good news about being five. As she tucked a message inside my purse, she told me I could start delivering messages on my own. I felt grown up as soon as I walked out the front door.

Everything went smoothly for the remainder of the year. On New Year's Eve we sat in the living room listening to Jack Benny and the Great Gildersleeve on the radio. Grampa said we would bang on pots at midnight to welcome the new year of 1945, but I fell asleep too early.

One day in January I went out to deliver a message near the top of the hill. I waved at a few friends building a snow fort, and they waved back. I loved that they knew I delivered important telephone messages.

Wind gusts swirled the new snow on the road into the random little piles. They were fun to jump on. A thin shell of ice beneath the soft snow popped each time I stomped.

I moved my purse forward to keep it from bouncing against my leg. Oh, what a terrible sight! The crease along the bottom of the purse had split open. I turned the purse upside down. Empty! The message was gone. When did this happen? *How* did this happen?

I spun around to look for the message. After a few steps I quickened my pace and scanned, radar-like, right to left and back again, hoping to see the paper gliding across the snow or to see it stuck on a frozen weed. With the wind constantly tweaking the snow and weeds, I realized it was gone. Frantic and desperate, I walked around in a circle, thinking about what to do.

With tears streaming down my cheeks and afraid to face my stern gramma, I started walking home. A car stopped behind me. I started running, stumbled, and fell face down. I did not know what would happen. I believed it would be bad.

Long strides crunched through the snow behind me. My heart beat faster and harder. Strong arms enveloped me from behind. I screamed. There was no escape. The arms picked me up off my feet and held me tight. My dad's voice asked, "Betty, are you hurt?"

Although happy to see him, I kept crying—not just drippy eyes, not just stifled moans, but loud sobs with huge tears. Dad lifted me into his truck, took out his big handkerchief, and dried my face. He removed my hat, patted my hair, and pulled me tight under his arm. Between sobs and gulps for air, I told him about the lost message. I sobbed hardest as I told him how much I feared telling Gramma.

Dad told me not to worry. He drove us home and explained to Mom, Gramma, and Grampa how it was just cold enough outside to make the plastic purse brittle. Gramma harrumphed. Even though she had heard the message hours ago, she recited it to Dad. He dashed out to make the delivery in his truck.

When he returned we ate supper, and not much later than usual, but in more silence. After losing the message and no longer having my purse, I felt too sad to speak.

Grampa and Dad sat in the living room smoking their pipes and listening to the evening news on the radio. Mom washed dishes and I dried. Gramma took advantage of the silence in the kitchen to criticize Mom and lecture me.

"It's not yer fault you lost the message. Yer mother shudda known if'n thar's a ice skim on a puddle, and the air's cold 'nuf to make a leaf brittle, then it's cold 'nuf to freeze a cheap plastic toy." Gramma blamed anything gone wrong on Mom. I later learned Gramma was jealous of Mom, because Mom had grown up in Phoenix and completed high school before marrying.

Grampa sometimes intervened when Gramma's criticisms seemed overly harsh. He would tell us, "Gramma's on her high horse, so just be quiet." He knew Gramma put Mom down to show us how sometimes experience trumps education.

But Grampa was not in the kitchen now and Gramma continued. "Who'd think a patent leather purse costed only a dollar?" She put scraps into the compost crock and started talking again before she fastened the lid. "And, Betty, you al'ays wanna answer the telephone, but you don't understand 'nuf words yet, and you can't write."

After we finished the dishes, Mom cheerfully changed the mood. "Who wants canned peaches?" she called.

Grampa and Dad came to the table as Gramma and I set out bowls and spoons. Better spirits prevailed as Mom ladled the peaches into the bowls. We smiled at each other with nearly every bite. Dad said people at work thought the war would end soon.

<hr>

The war ended before I started first grade in September 1945. From then on, Dad seemed to pinpoint everything as being "before the war or after the war." He started a new job in Flagstaff after Thanksgiving. We moved there before Christmas—to a house with a bathroom.

My new classmates did things I never imagined. They bought root beer barrels and wax lip candies at the corner store with weekly allowances, went to Saturday movies at the Orpheum, and from inside their homes they talked to each other on telephones.

Our home had the same black desk telephone as the other homes in our neighborhood. The front of all the phones had a piece of cardboard embedded in metal circle. That was where you found your telephone number. I learned to lift the Bakelite handset to listen for the dial tone and the operator who would say, "Number, please." If I picked up the receiver while someone else on our party line was talking, I'd hear their conversation. Because I remembered my gramma's strict orders, I always hung up immediately. ∾

Grandpa's Arizona Family

Gale Leach

The pavement ahead shimmered like water as we traveled east in my grandmother's 1957 Chevy. I flopped back on the seat, tired of waving my arm out the window, letting the wind push my palm back. Drops of sweat rolled down my neck. My mother said girls don't sweat, they perspire. Well, I was *sweating*, and we'd been on this road forever.

I wore a new dress my grandmother bought for this occasion. It was made of some crinkly material I hated before I even tried it on. It had that smell of unwashed cotton and the fabric was stiff, although the more I sweated, the softer it got. My shoes were new, too—black patent leather Mary Janes. I hated them more than the dress and wished I could have worn my jeans and sneakers. I looked like somebody else.

I lay down with my knees up, out of the sun. All I could see were clouds that looked like the drop biscuits my mom made. Once in a while there were scraggly tree branches and wires running from one telephone pole to another, curving down toward the middle and then up again at the next pole. Down and up. Down and up. Down and up.

I didn't mean to fall asleep. When I woke we'd arrived at my grandfather's new house in Phoenix. I sat up hoping to look out the window, but my grandmother pulled the front seat forward and leaned across me to get a bag. Her face was grim.

When I stepped out, my mother was waving to an old man who had come out of a pink stucco house. My grandfather looked just like the pictures I'd seen, with his bald head and laughing eyes. Grandpa walked toward us, hugged and kissed my mother and grandmother, and lifted me up into a hug. I was surprised— he was very short, and I was tall for my age. Hardly anyone ever lifted me up anymore. Even my mom told me I was too big to sit in her lap.

Grandpa set me down and said something in French. My grandmother's family had come from Canada, and my mom and Grandma spoke French when they called back east on Sundays and when they didn't want me to know what they were saying. I'd learned a few words, though, and I knew that Grandpa's mention of what sounded like "shun fig" meant young girl. I assumed he was talking about how tall I was. Everybody always did.

A younger woman came out of the house. I knew from pictures that this was my grandfather's new wife, Clarice. My grandmother said a lot of things about Clarice when my grandpa married her. Lots of them weren't too nice. Clarice was smiling, though, so maybe she wasn't so bad.

A girl in what also looked like a new dress followed Clarice. This was my aunt—not the woman, but the *child*. Candy had blonde hair, done in ringlets with ribbons. My short, brown hair had been permed for this occasion, but it refused to curl like hers, and no one would have gotten ribbons into it anyway.

"I'm Candy. I'm younger than you, but I'm your auntie! Isn't that funny?"

I stared down at her, not thinking it was funny at all. My mother's hand pressed onto my damp back, urging me forward. "Gale, go say hello."

"I'm Gale."

"I know. Wanna see my dolls? Daddy just bought me a new one that's *real*-ly special!"

"Gale, go play with Candy. We'll be eating soon," my mother said, ushering me down the walkway toward the house. I thought its pink color was a perfect match for Candy and her dolls and her dress. The last thing I wanted was to see a bunch of dolls, but I didn't have any choice.

I followed Candy inside and held the screen for my mom. Coming in from the bright sunshine, the room was dark. We'd entered the living room that had a couch and two chairs in front of a large wooden console that I knew must hold a big television. Candy turned down a hallway and I followed. The walls were covered with pictures, but I didn't get to really look at them. I did see one of Candy sitting on her mother's lap, and I wished I hadn't grown so tall.

We entered a room on the right. The walls were papered with a cutesy pattern of flowers in shades of pink and purple. Her bed had a puffy spread covered with more pink flowers. Some kind of gauzy fabric covered her headboard.

Candy led me to a wooden toy box, painted pink, of course. She pulled out a doll I recognized from commercials on TV as Chatty Cathy. If I had to play with a doll, this one wasn't bad. At least it did something.

"Wanna hear her talk?"

I nodded. Candy turned the doll over and pulled the string from her back.

"May I have a cookie?" Chatty Cathy asked, and I wondered how the voice worked. I wished I could take it apart.

Candy pulled the string a couple more times, and we listened as Chatty Cathy said, "Will you play with me?" and "I love you."

"Do you want to make her talk?" Candy asked, holding the doll out to me.

I took the doll and pulled the string. Instead of sliding back in, the string just hung there. Chatty Cathy said nothing.

"Oh, no!" Candy cried, snatching the doll from my hands. I felt myself turn red as I thought about getting in trouble for breaking her doll, even though it wasn't my fault and I hadn't done it on purpose. Candy ran into the hall crying and screaming, "Mommy! Mommy! Gale broke my doll!"

I followed, hoping I could explain what really happened, but Candy was already in her mother's lap whining about how I'd killed Chatty Cathy. I looked at my mother, knowing she'd know I hadn't done it on purpose, but it was still awkward. Clarice and my grandmother both glared at me. My mother looked caught in the middle, just like me.

"We'll pay for a new one," she said and motioned for me to sit next to her on the couch. I knew we didn't have much money, and I thought about my allowance being gone for the rest of my life to pay it back.

"I'm sorry about your doll," I said. My grandmother looked less stern then. Clarice was busy wiping tears from Candy's eyes.

"I'm sure Gale didn't mean to do it, Candy," my grandfather said. "I'll take care of it, Annette," he said to my mother. "Now, Gale, tell me what you like to do when you're not traveling to Arizona to meet your grandpa."

All eyes shifted back to me. I drew in a breath. "I like to sing and play softball. I like school. I want to be a scientist. I'll be in fourth grade next year."

"Fourth grade? I thought you were older!" Grandpa said. I liked that he thought I was older (most people did, because I was so tall,) but I also felt bad because he didn't know how old I really was.

"I'm eight."

"You can't be in fourth grade if you're eight," Candy said. "I'm seven, and I'm going into second."

"Gale skipped a grade," my mother said.

Candy glared at me. Clarice smiled, but it looked fake.

I squirmed as everyone looked at me again.

"Candy may skip a grade, too," Clarice said, beaming at her scowling daughter who was poking at Chatty Cathy's back trying to push the string back in. "Her teachers say she's very bright."

"Candy, why don't you take Gale outside and play?" my grandpa said.

"I don't want to."

"Candy, don't talk back to your father that way," Clarice said. I wondered if she ever reprimanded Candy like that when other people weren't around to hear it.

"I don't wanna go outside. It's too *hot!*" Candy whined.

"Just for a little while, until we go out to dinner. You can stay on the patio where it's not so warm."

Candy jumped down from Clarice's lap and ran to my

grandpa. Leaning against him, she whined, "Daddy, do I *have* to?"

"Candy, your mother said to go outside. Now go, and stay away from the pool." He gave her a pat on the bottom to usher her out.

Candy turned, glared at me again, and said, "Come on." She dropped the doll on the couch and headed outside. I followed.

We passed by the kitchen, and I was surprised to see that the appliances were all turquoise and looked brand new. I'd never seen appliances that were any color except white. Candy saw me looking and said, "Daddy just got those. They were really expensive. What color are *yours?*"

I thought of our kitchen with the knotty pine cabinets my father had made before he left and our white stove with some enamel chipped off near the bottom.

"We don't need appliances," I lied, knowing I'd probably get in trouble but unable to stop myself. "We always go out to eat. It's much nicer that way."

As we emerged from the back door, I felt a blast of heat. Candy's eyes widened, and then her face pinched. "That's not true. You're a liar."

I walked away from her and toward the pool that took up most of the backyard. It was very blue and had a slide with a waterfall, and the water looked cool. There was a pile of paving stones that still hadn't been laid over the dirt and gravel around one edge. "That's a nice pool," I said, trying to change the subject and avoid getting caught in the lie.

"Daddy got that for *me*," Candy said, and I believed her. I felt a stab of envy looking at the nice things Candy had, and I wondered why my grandparents got divorced and how come my grandpa had so much money. "Next week a teacher is coming to show me how to swim."

Not wanting Candy to one-up me, I said, "Swimming is fun. I swim in the ocean a lot. I'm going to learn to surf soon." Of course, the surfing was a lie. Some of my friends went surfing some times, but my mom said I was too young to go surfing. She wouldn't even let me have a bicycle because she was afraid I'd get hurt.

I knew Candy didn't believe my story, but she didn't make anything of it. "There's nothing to *do* out here," she said, pouting again. "We can't even play hide and seek because we don't have any trees."

She was right. Their yard inside the chain link fence was bare except for the rock and gravel that covered the dirt between and around the pool and patio. "Mommy doesn't want any leaves in the pool, so we're only going to have cactus and stuff."

"I never saw cactus like you have in Arizona until we came here. They're really huge and beautiful," I said, trying to be nice again.

"No, they're not. They're awful," Candy said, and I gave up trying to be nice. "All prickly and ugly," she continued. "I hate cactus. I wish we could go back to Massachusetts."

"You didn't used to live here?"

"No. We moved here in January. My parents wanted to get away from the snow."

Candy looked so sad, I almost started feeling sorry for her. I tried to think about what we could do that might be fun. "Do you have a ball? We could play here on the patio — like four-square, but only two."

Candy brightened. "Mommy just got one at the store. I'll get it."

While I waited, I glanced at the other houses I could see. Most of them looked new. The area where they lived was very flat. Some people had put fences around their yards, but most of the houses sat alone with nothing around them. No one had a lawn. Some had rock yards, some just dirt, and there were very few trees. There was lots of cactus, though, and the spaces between the houses had scrubby bushes and weeds. In the distance, the mountains looked like teeth.

Candy returned with a large, pink ball. We began bouncing it back and forth, and I started enjoying the game a bit. At least we were doing something and not just sitting around. Candy seemed to like it, too. We continued for a while until I hit the ball too hard. It rolled past Candy and stopped at the pile of paving stones. Candy ran to get it. She picked the ball up and turned around, but her new shoes must have slipped, because suddenly she was falling headfirst into the pool.

I ran over and watched her starched dress become soggy as her arms flailed. The ball floated away. Then I remembered she couldn't swim. I called out, "Grandpa! Grandpa! Come quick!" but no one came. I started to run back to the house when I saw Candy sinking beneath the water. I jumped into the pool.

I don't remember everything that happened next, but Candy's arms were everywhere and she kept going underwater. I know I finally pushed her to the edge of the pool and then up and over. After I climbed out, I ran back to the house and called through the door for everyone to come. Once they discovered what had happened, there was a huge commotion with people crying out and bringing towels and blankets and asking, "What happened?" and "Are you all right?"

With her bedraggled ringlets and ribbons plastered to her scalp, Candy was wrapped in a towel and coughing and sniffling in Clarice's arms. "We were playing ball, and I fell in the pool. Gale got me out."

I'd wondered if Candy was going to say I'd pushed her. She didn't, and I guessed she wasn't so bad after all. My mother wrapped me in a blanket and steered me toward the house and into the bathroom. Next thing I knew, I was dressed in some of Clarice's clothes while mine dried outside on the line.

When everything settled down, there was talk about me having saved Candy from drowning. I don't know if she would have drowned or not, but I enjoyed hearing people say nice things about me. Even Candy didn't seem too upset about that.

When things finally settled down, we began getting ready to go out to eat. As we headed toward the door, Chatty Cathy, lying alone on the couch, said, "I'm hungry." Candy ran back and grabbed the doll and I sighed, thinking maybe the trip to Arizona wasn't going to be quite so bad after all. ❧

The Shooting Match

Gale Leach

I stood under the soffit in front of the hotel, stealing what little shade it offered. I lifted my hat and wiped the sweat from my forehead. *One-Eye Willie must check the* Farmer's Almanac *and pick the hottest days to hold these shooting matches,* I thought.

It was only midmorning, but it was bound to be a scorcher. I wasn't the only one feeling the heat. Texas Jack leaned against the pole where some of the horses were tied and Hazel Green, in her tight corset, looked like she might faint. A cowboy rode through, his horse's hooves kicking up small clouds of dust that drifted in the dry air. Whatever didn't return to the road made a beeline for my clothes. Good thing I'd dressed like the men today, in saddle pants and boots. I dusted off my vest and replaced my hat.

I heard the familiar cadence of Sarsaparilla Sam's boots on the boardwalk behind me. My heart kicked up a notch. I didn't turn, pretending not to know he was there, and still I was startled when he reached around my waist and pulled me close. I could feel his breath and I could smell *him*, along with dried sweat and dust. Suddenly the heat didn't matter. The heat was inside. I wanted him, wanted him *now*.

"Didn't think I'd see you here," Sam said, turning me to face him and pushing my hat back from my face.

"Didn't expect to come. Young Joe brought me."

"Did he?" His brows lowered, and I noted a frown of jealousy as he took his arm away. Then, as quickly as it came, the frown was gone. "Did you come to watch me win?"

"I came to shoot." I pointed to my gun belt with two revolvers and the cart that held my shotgun and rifle. "I aim to win."

Sam threw his head back and laughed from deep within his chest. "Well, now, that's something. Cactus Kate, I hope you do!"

He held his elbow out, which I took in my own, and he walked me to my gun cart. He retrieved his own gear near the staging area, and when I approached he ushered me into line before him.

The competition would rotate us through what they called "stages." The first one for us was the barber shop. Iron targets were positioned at different distances behind the shop and each of us shot in a sequence, first with revolvers, then a shotgun, a rifle, and the shotgun again. Whoever hit the most targets in the fastest time won the stage.

I stood in line behind Two-Gun Tom who waited at the safety post where we loaded our guns before stepping up to shoot. The rest of us sweltered behind him in the sun hoping he was a fast shot so we'd be done sooner.

"You're lookin' good, Tom," said Galloping Grace, who was handling the safety table.

Tom smiled. "Gracie, you could make a cactus blush." He replaced his revolvers in his gun belt and moved to the shooting line.

"Good luck," she called as she watched him saunter, spurs jingling, toward the barber shop.

I moved up and laid my guns down, barrels pointed downrange, away from the participants. I opened the loading gates of my single-action Colt revolvers and cocked the hammers back enough to let the cylinders turn. I pulled ten bullets from my pouch and fitted them into the cylinders, five in each, leaving the last hole of the six-shooters empty beneath the trigger as a safety. Then I put ten bullets into my brand new 1866 Yellow Boy rifle, and I stuck four shotgun cartridges in my gun belt for quick access. All the while I could hear the "bang" and "ping" of Tom's bullets hitting the steel targets behind the barber shop. I loved shooting after Tom because his black-powder pistols made great clouds of sulfur smoke that smelled wonderful.

"Good luck to you, too, Kate," Gracie said as I holstered my pistols and carried the rifle and shotgun toward the barber's.

"Thanks, Gracie. I'll need it!" I said, hoping Sam's eyes were on my backside.

Justin Thyme had charge of this stage, and he gave me the instructions. "When Joe calls 'Go,' you say, 'Shave and a haircut, two bits.' Draw one pistol and shoot the far three targets from left to right to left. Then holster it and do it again with the other pistol. Load the shotgun and shoot the close targets in either direction. Drop the shotgun, grab your rifle, and shoot the targets on the hill, five shots on the left and five shots on the right. Drop the rifle, pick up and reload the shotgun, and shoot the close targets again. Drop the shotgun, raise your hands, and I'll call time. Got it?"

I thought I did but I'd found that, under pressure, it was easy to forget what you were supposed to do. If I shot the targets in the wrong order, that was as good as a miss, and a miss was five seconds off my time.

Nevertheless, I replied, "Got it." I laid my rifle on the table and set my shotgun against the wall.

"Are you ready?" Justin asked.

I nodded and raised my hands where everyone could see them.

"Go!"

I said my line and drew with my right hand, cocking the trigger as I aimed. Five shots—five pings—and I holstered that gun as I drew my left. I wasn't as fast left-handed, but I managed a good time with hits on all targets.

I shoved the pistol into its holster and reached for my shotgun. I broke it open, dropped a shell into each barrel and snapped the gun closed as I raised it toward the targets. Two hits later, I propped it against the wall and grabbed my rifle.

Of all my guns, I love the rifle best. It feels like part of me when I shoot, and I almost never miss. I knew I was nearly home free, now that I was clean to this point. I raced through the shots at the upper targets, set the rifle down, and grabbed the shotgun again.

I broke open the barrels, dropped the spent shells to the ground, and pulled the second set of cartridges from my belt, dropping them into the open barrels. I snapped the gun closed and pinged the last two targets.

"Great shooting, Kate," Justin said, beaming at me. Justin had been one of my early mentors when I was new to shooting.

"Thanks," I said, happy with the round. I could still feel Sam's eyes on me, or at least I hoped I could.

Justin turned to One-eye and asked the time.

"12.6 seconds," Willie said. "Clean. No misses."

I gathered my long guns and moved to the safety area beyond the barber shop where I laid them on the table for inspection. Coyote John looked them over, waved me on, and I carried them back to my cart.

The last of Sam's shots ring out in a fast staccato, and I heard Justin call "Time." I was sure he'd chosen the job of timekeeper because of his name. Joe said, "11.9 seconds, clean."

Damn, he'd beaten me again. Lots of shooters could do better — hell, some were so fast you couldn't hear the separate shots to count them — but that was a good time.

I watched as Sam cleared his guns through safety and brought them to his cart. He took off his hat and wiped his sleeve across his forehead, a gesture that was sexy when he did it, although it would have gone unnoticed by anyone else. Perhaps it was my heart and mind playing tricks.

"Good shooting, Kate," he said, settling his rifle and shotgun into their pockets.

"Yes, but you did better."

"So it's a competition between you and me, is it?" The corner of Sam's mouth turned up under his mustache.

"You'd like me to do well, wouldn't you?"

"Of course, but if you beat me what will you aspire to after that?"

"I'll figure out something," I said, smiling back at him.

"I'll tell you what — if you beat me today, I'll buy you dinner at Rosie's. If I beat you, you can cook for me at my place."

I didn't think I had a chance of beating him. I even thought about slowing down a little to ensure that I didn't. Dinner at his place sounded mighty nice. "You're on," I said. "No cheating now."

"Who, me?" He feigned an innocent look, raising his hands in the air. "I'm an officer and a gentleman by an act of Congress." He pointed to the red stripe running the length of his pants leg, which indicated Army artillery. Even more than shooting these guns, Sam loved to blow things up.

"I'll remember that," I said, and I started toward the second stage at the telegraph office.

The day progressed through hot and hotter, and my clothes became damp and my hair sticky. Still, I'd managed good times, and when Sam and I headed toward the jail, our last stage, I was only a little more than four seconds behind. I'd done well behind the bank, where the rifle targets were tough and Sam missed one. He'd beaten me at the saloon when I fumbled with my second pistol. If he missed a target here and I shot well, I had a chance to win. I counted twenty bullets into my pouch and put four more shotgun shells in my belt — always in the same place so they were easy to find when I needed them.

"Good luck," Sam said. He took me by the waist again, leaned forward, and kissed me. When he pulled away, he said, "I hope you win."

Surprised by the kiss, I blushed and felt a little flustered. "You're trying to make me lose my composure, Sam. Your tricks won't work. I'll see you when this is over."

He raised his hat and bowed as I wheeled my cart toward the jail. I loaded my guns and moved to the firing line. Dingo Dan explained the rules for this stage as I scanned the targets. Two down low for the shotgun, five further back for the pistols, and five spread out on the hillside for the rifle.

"When I say 'Go,' you reply, 'I've come to break you out, Dingo Dan,' and start shooting. Got it?"

I nodded and raised my hands to the ready position.

"Go!"

I made good time with both pistols, firing cleanly. I grabbed the shotgun, loaded two shells, and was rewarded with two loud pings as my shots met steel. I almost forgot the sequence for the rifle but caught myself in time. I set the rifle down, picked up the shotgun, emptied the barrels, and reached for the next two shells. My hand found nothing. I stared at my gun belt and saw empty slots where the shells should have been. They couldn't have fallen out — they were a fairly snug fit — but I looked around anyway, wondering if I could possibly have forgotten to load all four shells. No, I was certain I had them when I readied my ammunition.

Not wanting to take more time, I put the gun down and raised my hands. I'd be penalized ten seconds for missing the last two targets. Dan called, "Time," as he saw my hands go up. "Too bad, Kate. You won't forget them next time."

"I didn't forget them *this* time," I grumbled, wondering where they'd gone. As I stepped away from the firing line, Dan said, "10.6 seconds, plus two misses, for a total of 20.6." I collected my long guns and headed toward the safety table. I laid my guns out for inspection and thought about the round.

I wasn't upset about losing to Sam. I looked forward to cooking for him. But I was stumped trying to figure out how I could have been so forgetful, still believing I had loaded four shells. *Let it go,* my mind decreed, and I concentrated on listening for Sam's score. As I placed my guns in the cart, I heard Dan say, ". . . with three misses, for a total of 27.1 seconds."

That couldn't be right. I turned and spotted Sam heading toward the safety table, a sheepish grin on his face. Even his mustache couldn't hide that smile.

When he'd finished the safety check, he wheeled his cart beside mine and smiled again. "I guess you win, Cactus Kate. Looks like I'll be taking you to Rosie's for dinner."

"I didn't win," I said, looking up at those blue eyes again. "You threw the match. Couldn't stand the idea of my cooking, huh?"

He slipped his arm around my waist again and gave me a squeeze. Again, I started to feel the flush that had nothing to do with the afternoon sun. When he pulled back, he looked me up and down and said, "I thought you forgot those last two shells," as he pointed to my belt.

I looked and there they were, right where they should have been before. Then it clicked. Sam had removed them when he hugged me before the last stage. He'd replaced them just now when he hugged me again. I started to fume when I caught myself and realized he'd just been playing with me, which is why he'd forfeited the match.

"You were so darned serious, I couldn't help but have a little fun, Kate. Hope you're not mad."

Whatever anger I had disappeared when I saw the twinkle in his eyes. "I thought I was going crazy for a while. So we'll never know who would have won, not really."

He looked at me, long and steady. "I know who won," he said, and his smile returned. "Cactus Kate, let's go home."

I nodded. "I need to get my regular clothes from Joe's car," I said, heading toward a silver Hyundai. Pulling them out of the back seat, I piled my blue jeans, t-shirt, and tennis shoes on top of my gun cart and wheeled it back toward our pickup. "I like calling you Sam," I said. "It fits you better than Richard, at least when we're totin' guns for Cowboy Action Shooting. Maybe we should keep these personas full-time and change our names."

He smiled but shook his head, as he hoisted our gun carts into the truck and closed the tailgate. "No. I like you as Kate, but I married you as Gale, and I'm too fond of modern conveniences to give them up for this kind of life. That is, unless you want to go home, fire up that wood stove, and get me my vittles."

"No such luck," I said. "You're taking me to Rosie's, remember? I'm ordering a hamburger, a wonderfully modern dish."

———◦◦◦———

Author's Note: My husband and I are members of the Single Action Shooting Society (SASS), an international organization created to preserve and promote the sport of Cowboy Action Shooting.™ SASS endorses regional matches conducted by affiliated clubs, stages the World Championship of Cowboy Action Shooting (called "End of Trail"), promulgates rules and procedures to ensure safety and consistency in Cowboy Action Shooting matches, and seeks to protect its members' Second Amendment rights. SASS members share a common interest in preserving the history of the Old West and competitive shoot-ing. Each participant must adopt a shooting alias and costume appropriate to a character or profession of the late 19th century. Many event participants gain more enjoyment from the cos-tuming aspect of the sport than from the shooting competition itself. SASS events provide regular opportunities for fellowship and fun with like-minded folks and families. ∾

The Wrong-Way Quail

Gale Leach

"Stop, stop! There's something in the road!"

My husband was used to my asking him to pull over when I spotted an interesting tree or a house I wanted to photograph. Sometimes he'd stop without a fuss; sometimes he'd give me that look—the one that says, "I'll indulge you again, but you owe me." This time, he knew something more was going on than just sightseeing, and he applied the brakes just in time, stopping the car a few feet in front of a tiny Gambel's quail running in circles on the road.

I opened the door, signaled to a driver approaching behind us in the other lane to stop, and then tried to circle around behind the baby bird, urging him with my outstretched arms to go back to the curb. Each time I'd get near him, he'd run the other way. My husband told me later he wished he'd had a camera to capture the sight of a tall woman bent over in the middle of the road with her arms spread wide, chasing after a quail the size of a cotton ball.

I couldn't understand why the little bird was running in circles except that perhaps his feet were too hot. It was in the hundreds that day, as it often was during late May in Arizona. I'd heard that dogs could get their paws burned walking on hot pavement, so perhaps that was it. Then again, maybe he was just crazy with the loss of his family. There were no other quail anywhere around that I could see.

I was finally able to grab the quail, and I deposited him on the pathway beyond the road hoping he would head wherever he belonged. Of course, he headed right back into the road, running in circles.

I chased him again, getting winded now. When I eventually caught him once more, I motioned for my husband to open my car door. He pushed it open, I climbed inside, and he reached around me to pull it closed and drove off.

"What are you going to do with it?" he asked, using that tone of voice that's always the same whenever I do something like this. This wasn't the first time. I don't mean to bring things home. It just happens.

My first foray into the world of raising wild creatures was years ago, before we moved to Arizona. I'd found a baby mockingbird that had fallen from its nest. It was still a nestling—not yet fully feathered—and I couldn't locate any nests nearby. I called various wildlife agencies to determine the best course of action. Taking their suggestions, I created a new nest made from a bowl lined with twigs, some quilt batting, and strips of cotton cloth and tied this to a branch near where I'd found the bird. I waited for most of a day, but when there was no sign of a parent visiting the nest I retrieved the bowl and brought the little bird inside.

I knew the bird needed live food, so I bought meal worms and baby crickets from the pet shop. I placed the nest in the bowl of a standing floor lamp thinking the little guy would be warmer up high. Using tweezers, I picked up a worm and held it near the bird. I rubbed it on his beak.

Nothing. He just lay there, looking weaker. I knew I had to get him to eat or he'd die.

I tried everything. I poked him, stroked him, lifted his beak—nothing. I began to despair that I'd lose him after all. I tried again and again, with the same result. Finally, upset that nothing was working, I rapped on the bowl of the lamp. His beak flew open, and he began to chirp. I grabbed the tweezers, pulled a mealworm from the container, and popped it into his mouth.

He swallowed that and resumed chirping, mouth open. I fed him I-don't-know-how-many worms until his head sagged back down, and he settled in for a rest. If he didn't die of overeating, I thought he'd make it.

I learned later that what triggered him to open up was when he thought Mom had landed on the nest. Every time I wanted to feed him all I had to do was tap on the edge of the lamp, and his mouth would pop open.

He wasn't so keen on the worms, although he liked the crickets. Even better were the black water beetles I found in the recess of the water meter outside. I learned that I could stun a beetle, bring it inside in a margarine tub, and feed it to him whole. These weren't small beetles, and it sometimes took a little doing for me to get all the legs in his mouth and for him to swallow it. We named him "Griz" because of this grizzly taste in food.

Griz lived with us for several weeks while he fledged, and we taught him to peck fruit, find seeds, and hunt for bugs. I had to work during the day, so I'd leave him in the house with a window open. After work he was never inside, so I'd go to the back porch and call his name. He'd chirp in reply, often from quite a distance. I'd call again and his chirp would be closer, until finally Griz would sail down and land on my arm. It was an amazing feeling to have a semi-wild bird come to me. I was both honored and awed.

We had been preparing to move for some time, and we finally put the house up for sale. We needed to travel to Arizona to look for our new home, so we asked our real estate agent to watch for Griz and put food out for him when she came to the house, just in case he needed it. Sadly, she reported that she never saw him during any of her visits, and when we returned my calls were answered with silence. Either he'd also moved on or something worse had happened. I preferred to think he'd found a female friend, and that they, too, had gone on to start a new life.

The success in raising Griz led me to believe that I could be of help to other creatures that later ended up with me. One of the first in Arizona occurred when a friend returned a portable sewing machine she'd borrowed, and I discovered that a momma mouse had delivered a nest of babies inside the bobbin area. What could I do? Kill them? True, I'd been known to put out mouse traps in the past, and I hadn't felt qualms about that (or at least not many,) but those were unknown mice. These were *my* mice in *my* sewing machine. I managed to raise those mice to the point where they were old enough to make their own way, or so I hoped.

My husband said I'd reared them to the point where I could now catch them in traps if they got in the house, but I ignored him.

Another time, it was a whole nest of baby birds. My husband and I had driven to the storage facility to get our fifth-wheel trailer as we prepared for a trip. As my husband backed the truck toward the trailer, I heard a "cheeping" coming from the hitch. Fifth-wheel hitches are large metal contraptions that have an open area behind the actual connector. Peering inside, I could see that a bird had roosted inside that space. I reached in and pulled out a nest of baby birds that were definitely too young to fly. We decided it would be best to put the nest somewhere up high so the parents might find it and the babies wouldn't be eaten. We managed to attach it to a chain-link fence under the eaves of a building, and we left on our trip knowing we'd done what we could.

Two days later, at our final campsite, we unhitched the truck and again heard cheeping. I looked inside the hitch and discovered a second nest I'd missed earlier. Of course, there was no hope that mama bird would come to feed these babies, so out came the nest and into the trailer it went. My husband gave me another of those looks—the one where his eyes roll upward and his mouth makes a straight line. I was fairly used to it. We'd been married for a while.

The issue was more than what to feed them. I was pretty sure I could figure that out, and it turned out that an ear syringe worked pretty well to deliver bits of canned dog food mixed with water. The problem was how to keep the two cats that had traveled with us from eating the birds before we could get them back home. We managed it by sequestering the birds in the bathroom shower, and they thrived during the week we were there. By the time we reached home they were close to fledging, and after another few days we delivered all four of them to a woman in Phoenix who rescues finches. My smug smile that day was definitely a match for my husband's eye-rolling smirk.

Another time I was in the outdoor garden section at the hardware store, and I heard what I thought was yet another baby bird chirping from beneath a display of seed packages. It was calling very loudly. I thought that was strange, based on what I'd learned with Griz. Using a stirring stick procured from the paint department, I swiped under the seed display and dislodged not a baby bird but a baby vole. (I didn't know that then; it looked just like a gray baby mouse with a lot more fur.) You can guess the rest. After borrowing a paper cup from someone in the store, I scooped up the baby, took him home, and eventually let him go in the backyard when I was sure he was old enough to survive. My husband made more comments about my having raised yet another plaything for the cats.

Now, I had a baby quail in my hands, we had *three* cats at home, and I had no idea how to care for it. I knew quail were different from other birds. I thought I'd read that they didn't even nest but had their babies on the ground underneath bushes. What would I do with this tiny feathered thing?

After making our way in the house, I held the bird while my husband opened one of our cat carriers and placed it on top of the dryer in our laundry room. I put the quail inside and zipped it up. In an ironic sort of turnaround, the cat carrier seemed to be the only thing we could think of that would keep the quail safe from the felines.

I learned from the internet that quail do make nests lined with grass, leaves, and feathers, usually concealed by foliage. I also learned that quail babies need to be warm, so we put a heating pad beneath the carrier and added a soft rag inside that I thought the bird might like to snuggle against. One article said that even the tiniest quail eat seeds, so I scattered some bird seed on the floor of the carrier, closed the laundry room door, and hoped for the best overnight until I could take the quail out in the morning.

Gambel's quail don't have families like other birds. They co-mingle in groups, but if they are separated from one group they usually join another. That was good news for this little quail. I determined to head toward the local golf course where I'd seen lots of quail in the past and get him acquainted with his new family.

The next morning my husband and I made several trips, only to find absolutely no quail. They'd simply disappeared. Of course, I'd never charted their patterns, and I'm sure it was simply a matter of poor timing on our part that we kept missing them.

We scouted around a bit during the day and still no sign of any quail. Finally that evening before dinner we made another foray to the golf course and this time found many quail darting in clumps and lines from one place to another.

We took the carrier to the top of a small hill where I hoped the little quail could see the others. I opened the zipper and tried to get him to move, but he stood rooted at the very back of the carrier. Eventually, I reached in and grabbed him again.

I set him on the grass and he began running, but he headed directly *away* from all the groups of quail and toward a house near one of the greens. At that moment I thought that if I'd had plans to name him I would surely have chosen Corrigan, since he always went the wrong way.

In what was getting to be a habit I chased after him and tried to block his path, like a cowboy coaxing a stray calf back to the herd. Eventually the tiny quail turned and must have seen the others as he headed toward them with abandon (or perhaps he was just terrified of me, but either way it worked.)

Out of breath again, but happy the saga of the little bird would have a happy ending, we headed home. I could see the edges of a smile beneath my husband's moustache too, although he'd never admit it. ∾

Thirst

Justin Lloyd

Turtles. Here? I look around for a house. Anything explaining this oasis surrounded by rocky desert and scrub-brush. My tired call into the void is met with only a diminishing echo. The concrete trough full of water rests alone in the mountains. Green algae cling to decayed sides, belching bubbles of gas through the water. Two red-eared sliders swim comfortably in the parched and beautiful wasteland. It has been hours since I saw another soul.

My hand breaks the shimmering surface. Ripples disturb the balance. Water drops over the broken edge, slowly seeping into the cracked ground screaming for more. The trickle barely quenches Mother Earth's thirst as the wind whisks the moisture away. With a deep breath the serenity I sought for months enters my lungs.

The sun drifts behind the jagged horizon casting orange and pink hues through the atmosphere. I set up camp for the night under a cluster of trees towering above the dry yellow grass. A fallen tree trunk rests on the sandy swath near the charred remains of unknown adventures. Encircled by rocks, the pit is ready to burn into the night. Symbolizing man's control over nature, fire connects me to humanity's Neolithic roots. Warmth. Light. Protection. Smoke slows the swarms of flies. Flames discourage herds of curious javelin; short and muscular, their tusks protrude downward like daggers from leathery snouts. I unscrew the blue clasp on the scuffed bottle dangling from my backpack. The temperature of the wind tastes pure as a crystal winter spring.

Exhausted from climbing mountains and descending into valleys, my muscles ache and patches of skin are scraped red from thorny plants spilling over the trails. Roaming miles of hard ground batters the bones. I gather firewood and clumps of dried grass. A flick of my thumb ignites the small bundle of grass and twigs. Festering tinder becomes logs erupting with flames. Pop. Sizzle. Pop. Pop. Moisture locked deep inside the logs boils while flames burn with wavering light. Apples, canned chicken, granola, and a bottle of water fill my stomach. The cloudy sky obscures the moon and stars while crickets chirp rhythmically against the pall of night. The desert hums with the swarms of insects rising into the cooling night air from the blades of wild-grass. Troubles disappeared earlier when I walked quietly through the beautiful canyons and peered over mountains.

My eyes stare into the tangoing flames. Forgotten problems cascade into a furious kaleidoscope of consciousness. I rub my face with disappointment. The log reduces to a smoldering glow as I drift to sleep.

Minutes limp forward as I clean my desk. Four-thirty, reports filed. Four-forty, appointments logged. Pens neatly placed inside a black metal cylinder. I stare blankly at the computer screen, waiting for five o'clock to end the trite work week. The hours, like my career, are stagnant inside this morally knotted machine. Drifting through time only on momentum. Fingers pound keys daily, while I hide the disdain buried inside. Breads and circuses have us chasing the dreams of rabbits. Forty hours of anguish each week. Racing through the muck to live freely for two days. Unsure who we all are, I yearn to break from the trappings of the life I have crafted. With middle-class guilt I feign productivity as my boss walks around the corner.

"Can I see you a moment?"

A simple nod of the head, and I walk toward her office. I pass cages equipped with humming computers and beeping phones, each filled with unrealized potential. I step into a meeting. An ambush. By the time it is over I walk into an empty cavern.

Fired. Released from the polyester prison enveloping each passing week. I exit the cold building and walk through the parking lot to my car standing alone. I place the small box of pictures on the backseat. Unsure of what is next, I drive home through the dark avenues.

———◦◦———

My eyes open as raindrops roll from my nose to the corners of my mouth. The shower reverberates off leaves above. No shelter and I panic in the rain. My heart pumps. Thoughts of racing through the darkness to my car converge into a dozen scenarios exploding through my mind. My pulse slows and my head cools. With all my belongings secure inside my backpack, I realize the rain is barely coming down. I slide inside my sleeping bag with only my face exposed. I quickly fall asleep inside the feathery cocoon.

Cool morning air refreshes my bare chest. The evidence of rain has all evaporated. I reach into my backpack for canned pineapple. I sit on the log, eating, while listening to a handful of birds call through the trees. The warm coals still glowing orange hiss as I release yesterday's excess on the fire pit. My hand plunges into the miniature oasis, disturbing the tranquility of the oblivious turtles.

Water fills an empty plastic bottle. I pour it over the ash and coals, extinguishing the campfire. With two large bottles of water and the few ounces of pineapple juice saved from breakfast, I trek through the immediately familiar shrubs. My focus drifts home and my troubles ahead. My wilderness reprieve is ending. I feel like a comet spiraling to an inevitable collision.

———◦◦———

Cold and dry, our home has withered to an urban desert of humanity. Divorce lingers over a slowly rotting relationship. Misery without a breaking point. For the sake of the children we remain under the same roof but sleep in different rooms. The farce we call living just delays our inescapable future. We wait with indifference for this charade to end, releasing the uncomfortable tension casting a shadow into each corner. Nothing is wrong or right, merely sharing space as we proceed with our days. Not without love but rather an absence of fondness. Like old acquaintances we pass through the corridors unsure if we should acknowledge one another.

Monday I drove toward the mountains with numb indifference. Indifferent to the loss of my job. Indifferent to my home. Indifferent to living. Not suicidal. Lost in life. Ashamed, I clung to silence through the weekend, waiting to unburden myself with the truth. Disgust and disappointment are sure to follow news of my joblessness. Failure. Lies of vacation days to go camping. That is the story I told. Instead there is no place to be. The note said I would be home around noon on Tuesday. Time alone to sort my situation out, but I know there is no answer.

———⊃◦⊂———

I walk over the same dried river-bottoms as the day before. Marked by stacked rocks, trails reconnect on the other side. Are these different? Beds lined with millions of grey stones rounded by ancient rushing waters, all look identical. Every direction of the barren wilderness is scarred by these ancient rivers.

My shattered life flashes across my eyes. The trail fails to reconnect as I reach the dried bank. I turn around. Was I even on a trail? Nothing looks obvious. Carelessly, I meandered through the open desert to a riverbed just like the ones I crossed yesterday.

After a few slugs of water I follow the river bottom south, climbing over dead trees sun-bleached and scattered by flash floods. The sun dampens my face. A lizard darts over the rocks, retreating to a hidden patch of shade. Traveling the land unsure of myself, I reach a trail with no name. No map, and the handwritten directions are worthless. I walk along the trail under the guise I will see something familiar. Hubris is a sin against nature.

After hours of walking under the sun, my body is tired, hot, and thirsty. The trail widens into an open plateau. The ghosts of horses emboss the dusty mesa. Prickly pear cactus are scattered around the perimeter. A single tree stands to my left. I walk over the ridge and peer into the great nothingness. The trail narrows into a small passage leading to mountains and desert until the peaks turn purple.

The midday sun continues heating my body, and my mouth is dry. I reach into my bag, and only a few ounces of water remain. The turtles swim in gallons and gallons of bountiful liquid. I take a swig. Hot as the morning sun, the water tastes delicious meeting my dry lips. My location is a mystery. Only one drink remains, and I am still thirsty.

Open and elevated. This is the location for my final stand. The ground next to the tree is soft enough and the shade is cool. I unroll my sleeping bag and drift to sleep. Twenty minutes or two hours?

My eyes open. The thirst is taunted by the last drops inside my canteen. Images of someone finding my brittle, mummified corpse are juxtaposed by the nightmare of my daughters losing their father forever. I sense madness and panic would overtake me in the final hours of dehydration.

Under the shade, I wait for anyone passing by. I drift between mortality and the mundane as night falls. Stars twinkle as airplanes glide through the sky unaware of the terror below. I call out my daughters' names with tempered fear. Fear I may never hug them again.

"Jasmine. Renee."

My fatigued voice replies. Wonder replaces fear as I peer into the dark rift cutting through the galaxy. Merely a point on a planet, I gaze with awe into what appears to be specks of light, years away. The ancients viewed these fields of stars separated by unfathomable distance without the smog and fluorescents masking the infinite above. Mentally exhausted I fall asleep. Repeatedly through the night I alter between the horror of consciousness and the comfort of dreams. The stars and moon shifting over the horizons is my only reference for time.

The sun emerges through the distant peaks. I awaken, oblivious to the miserable scent I exude inside the warmth of my sleeping bag. The cool air does not refresh like yesterday. I piss into an empty bottle and gaze at the orange liquid with morbid curiosity. On the sandy open patch I spell "Help" with rocks before it gets hot. I collect dead wood and anything that will burn. Green branches erupt into thick plumes rising into the empty sky. Smoke to signal someone, anyone, I am here.

I light the fire and wave a red bandana as planes and helicopters fly by. Again and again I repeat this fruitless process. Under the palo verde tree I sit slumped, merely an unnoticed grain in a sea of sand. The sun heats the ground, and the shade begins to feel hot. My parched body cannot produce tears as I think of hugging my daughters. With my hands clasped around my face I tell Jasmine and Renee I love them.

My knife digs into the arm of a saguaro cactus. Dragging the blade down a few inches I cut a hole, searching for a well of sterile liquid. Disappointment follows. I cut off a cladode from a prickly pear cactus. Slowly under the shade I pluck the spines from the flat green cactus paddle using the needle-nose tool on my Leatherman. I cut the cactus into chunks and place it inside a small plastic bag. I pound the sealed bag with a rock until the cactus paddle is an unrecognizable mash. The pittance of juice tastes how I would imagine the flavor of aloe vera lotion. The effort is worthless.

Thirst controls everything as a Cessna flies in the distance. I light my fire. Green cactus burns. Thick plumes billow into the sky. The smell of smoke overtakes all my clothes. Unnoticed again. Beads of sweat drip from my temple as I retreat to the shade. I look at the horseshoe prints scattered along the wide and open trail. How old are they? A day? A week? When will someone cross my path? My head droops with failure. This failure is real and not conjured by insecurity and self-doubt.

Wind blows across the mesa shuffling the gravel and lifting the dirt. My head hangs with anguish as my back rests against the tree. A woman appears. Elation. Relief. Survival. I shout an unrecognizable garble of words. I try again. "I'm so glad to see you." A rush comes through me as I know my life is not ending in a parched whimper. The woman is puzzled.

"I got lost and ran out of water yesterday."

"Are you okay? Can you walk?"

"Yeah, just thirsty."

"Drink this slowly. My car's 'bout two miles down the trail."

The first gush of water hitting my lips feels like life. We walk over the mountains. I quench my thirst slow and steady. Once we reach her car I dial home. My wife answers with an emotionally drained "Hello." It is obvious she has been crying and has not slept much.

"A hiker found me. I love you."

"I love you too." ∾

Browned Flour

Jessie Swierski

Esther, a young woman where I worked, was expecting her first child. We enjoyed a lot of conversations, and she talked about her hopes and fears for her son. As her due date approached, I started thinking about baby gifts. I knew I could get the usual stuff—diapers, clothes, blankets, etc. Those options didn't really satisfy me, because I knew she would get those from everyone.

During one conversation Esther and I talked about the everyday care that newborns require, and she mentioned wanting to avoid diaper rashes. I knew right away what my gift would be. I would give her the gift I was blessed to receive twenty-five years ago, when I was a young mother.

When she opened the bag, it would not have surprised me if she'd said, "This is weird!" She's too polite to do that, but she might have thought it when she pulled out the jar of browned flour. I told Esther to read the story that goes with the jar.

In April of 1988, Mike and I moved from El Paso, Texas, to Phoenix. We were traveling with our young daughter, Alysa. She was six months old when we made the drive in our yellow VW Bug. We did everything we could to be the perfect parents. We read books, went to classes, interviewed pediatricians, and made sure she received the best of everything.

As first-time parents, Mike and I went overboard in caring for Alysa. Every time she would get a little dirty, she was cleaned up and redressed. Despite all of our zeal, Alysa ended up with a diaper rash. I ran right out and bought cream to treat it—after crying, of course.

The cream didn't work. Next Mike and I tried a gel. That didn't work. We tried letting her walk around without a diaper for several hours a day. That didn't work. We tried giving her multiple baths a day, but that only dried out her skin. I read everything I could get my hands on about how to treat diaper rashes. Somewhere along the way I heard or read about other parents who swore that using a black light would work. Mike and I were so desperate we tried it. Alysa would take a nap on my lap, and I would open her diaper and hold a black light over her bottom the entire time she was sleeping.

It didn't work.

We took her to her pediatrician. He said to change her diaper frequently and use rash creams. That visit frustrated us, because he didn't tell us anything we hadn't already tried. Feeling discouraged, I headed out to buy more cream. I felt so bad for Alysa, because she was just miserable. Of course, I felt Mike and I were doing this whole parenting thing wrong.

As I stood and read package after package, a tiny old lady asked me what I was doing. She startled me, because I never heard her walk up. I told her I was trying to decide what cream to try next because my daughter had a diaper rash that wouldn't go away.

This little old woman was shorter than five feet and very thin. Her eyes, a deep brown, looked calm and wise. She wore a long dress and a hat. She asked, "Don't you know about browned flour?"

"No. I've never heard of browned flour."

"Child, take some flour, put it in a pan, and cook it on low heat. Keep turning and stirring it until it turns a light, golden brown. Then, after you let it cool, put some of that flour on the baby and clear up that rash."

I told her I would try it and said thank you. I was so desperate to help Alysa I didn't think twice about trying the browned flour. I thought about buying another box of rash cream just in case the flour remedy failed. I don't know why, but I put down the boxes of cream in my hand. When I looked up, the woman had disappeared as quickly and silently as she had appeared. I went down the baking aisle, picked up a bag of flour, paid for it, and left the store.

After I got home, I told Mike about the conversation I had with the old woman. He was skeptical about trying a home remedy and was a little irritated that I had come home without any diaper rash creams. I put the flour in a pan and cooked it until it was a beautiful golden color. After it cooled I changed Alysa's diaper and applied a light dusting of the flour to her bottom. Two hours later I changed her diaper again.

I saw a difference in that short amount of time. Her bottom had gone from a dark, angry red to a bright red. I applied another light dusting of the flour and kept on changing her every two to three hours. By the next morning she only had a few bumps, and her color was almost back to normal. Mike was amazed and became a believer in this home remedy.

By the next day, Alysa was completely better. I don't know the science behind this remedy, but I do know this treatment came along when I knew there was nothing else we could do. I had prayed that God would help, and when I felt hopeless that little old woman showed up. I don't know if she was an angel, but her advice answered my prayers.

I never saw that old woman again, so I never had a chance to tell her how grateful I was for her advice. I honor her now by sharing her advice with other new mothers.

I had given Esther two outfits, a bath-time book, a jar of browned flour, and, of course, the story behind it. She said later that the story was her favorite gift. I told Mike about the gifts I had given to Esther. He laughed and said now I was the old lady sharing stories.

That's okay by me. ∾

Arizona Blue

Jessie Swierski

There's nothing like the brilliant blue of Arizona's summer days, and today was no exception. I knew today promised to be another beautiful day. The sky was a clear, bright blue with a few light clouds visible far off on the horizon. The sunshine felt warm as it caressed my left arm through the window of the truck, and I found myself feeling grateful that the scorching summer heat wasn't making its presence felt quite yet.

My stomach was tense, and as I gripped the steering wheel with fingers slightly aching from stiffness, I frantically tried to read the freeway signs. Kayla, my younger daughter, kept telling me to calm down and that everything would be all right. After passing N. Verrado Way, I knew we had gone too far. If I didn't turn around soon, the next stop would be California. Getting off the freeway, Kayla and I meandered through a couple of neighborhoods before finally finding a road that allowed us to head north instead of west. Once again we were on our way to meet the rest of the family.

Kayla was a rock during the drive, and I still remember how calm she was while I was the one feeling frantic and out of control. I looked at her and realized that somewhere along the way my baby girl had grown into an awesome, knowledgeable, accomplished young woman. It was nice to know I could count on her instead of always being the one to do the comforting. I didn't know how I would feel later, so I felt determined to capture as many enjoyable moments as I could. As I pulled into the lot, my heart began to feel heavy with the knowledge that today was really the day when I had to say goodbye. We had all arrived for the same purpose, and I think Geno would have been happy knowing his family was together again . . . even if it was for an occasion such as this.

Mike, my husband and the oldest son, and Alysa, our elder daughter, were already in the parking lot. Jeff, the middle son, and Andy, the youngest son, and Mike, all received a small portion of Geno's ashes in the keepsake containers they had brought along. This was the first time in a while all three sons had gotten together to share an occasion. I found it bittersweet that it took this sad circumstance to bring them together. It was also the last time they would be together in the foreseeable future. Jeff and his wife, Vicki, along with Andy, his wife, PennyLane, and their children, Javier, Tiana, and Geszer had all come to share in this event.

We started out on the hike, all in agreement that this was the right decision. Geno had loved the weather here in Arizona and had expressed his desire to remain a part of the Arizona landscape for all time. He especially loved this park, often marveling at the wide variety of beauty that made up the desert landscape. The crunch of the gravel lent a welcome break in the awkward silence that we kept trying to break with superficial chatter, pointing out this bit of green or that small animal print. I didn't know if there were any rules of etiquette one should observe, and apparently I wasn't the only one without that knowledge. We all worked hard to make sure nothing unpleasant was brought up. This wasn't the time to be hashing out differences.

After hiking for about a half-hour, Mike and his brothers began the task of deciding where Geno would rest. While they would make the final decision, everyone piped in with an opinion. I ended up taking pictures from different angles and a variety of areas. I wanted to get a picture of Geno's place of rest, so the location needed to make a nice picture.

The final resting spot was nestled on the north side of some large boulders, ringed on both sides by young palo verde trees. To the west of the area we saw some tall saguaro cacti that seemed to stand guard over the chosen location. This area screamed Geno, so making the final decision seemed like it just waited to be discovered by us.

Jessie Swierski

After everyone agreed to this location we stood there in a half circle, shuffling our feet and making furtive eye contact with one another. No one knew quite how to proceed. Mike took the ashes and walked towards the boulders. Taking the lid off the canister he held it in both hands and began to turn, allowing the ashes to pour out onto the ground. A slight breeze blew some of the ashes back into Mike's face, causing him to cough a little. Thanks to that breeze he now wore some of the ashes, almost like Geno had given him one last caress. Watching some of the ashes float away, I wished Geno well on his journey. As Mike tried to brush some of the ashes away and finish spreading the ashes we all chuckled at his dilemma, grateful for the brief respite from this solemn occasion.

Mike joined us at the entrance to Geno's resting place, and again we all wondered how we should proceed. Vicki, Jeff's wife, suggested that we all share one of our favorite memories of Geno. Sharing our stories seemed like a great idea, and I think everyone was glad to share something happy. The temperature started to heat up, so everyone shared the brief version of their stories.

Andy had the same lighthearted sense of humor Geno often displayed. He began teasing Alysa, and she matched him wit for wit. I'm not sure how it happened, but as we began walking Alysa threw a small rock at him and hit him on the top of his head. I think her accuracy surprised him. Their play provided another nice break from the emotional turmoil we all tried to keep in check.

We continued our way back towards the parking lot and said our goodbyes, promising we would not let so much time and distance come before our next gathering. On some sad level, I think we all knew those were just the polite platitudes people often speak with sincerity that lingers only for the moment.

As Kayla and I got in the truck and started heading home, I thought back to the first time I ever met Geno. That first meeting, so long ago, set the course for our beautiful and rocky friendship.

Thinking about that first meeting, on September 19, 1986, in El Paso, Texas, the memory was so clear it seemed like yesterday.

I had spent most of the day preparing the meal for our rehearsal dinner, and cleaning up afterwards took longer than expected. The kitchen of the church felt smaller than it actually was, and I ended up with wet spots on my clothes from washing dishes and putting away food. Time became my enemy, because it stole the opportunity to make myself presentable before rushing to the airport to meet my future in-laws. The air itself felt heavy and stifling as I tried to still the flutters of nervous tension radiating within my stomach. Mike rode to the airport with the Craig, his best man, and the other Craig, a groomsman nicknamed the Viking.

As I stood in the waiting area Mike came rushing up to me and said that Craig the Viking was being arrested after mouthing off to a police officer who told him he couldn't park in a specific spot. All I could think was, "You have got to be kidding me!" Mike made a speedy introduction that sounded like, "Here are my parents, this is Michelle. Her name is Jessie Michelle, but since her dad's name is Jesse, go ahead and call her Michelle," and then he rushed off to bail the Viking out of jail while I stood there in stained clothes, messy hair, and a sweaty face about to meet my future in-laws. Great, this was just the beginning I was hoping for—not! This new development did not help my churning stomach.

As I turned to meet Geno and Lucy, I found myself staring at Geno's stomach. I looked up and up some more until I saw his smile and twinkling eyes. He was a big bear of a man, easily clearing six feet, and he had a full beard and mustache covering his face. He said, "Hi, Michelle," and gave me a big hug. Then he held out a paper bag and told me to be careful with it, because it contained a live present for me.

I still chuckle every time I remember my feeling of trepidation upon looking in the bag. Inside were two young, scrawny maple trees Geno brought from Pennsylvania. Alas, they didn't survive life on my balcony in El Paso, but the memory of Geno's gift still makes me smile. Thinking about Geno's gift, offered so many years ago, helped to ease the sorrow of saying goodbye.

I felt a nice sense of relief and gratitude for all my memories. Geno's open acceptance was a gift that would last for the duration of our shared time. He offered me his friendship, and though there were times when our friendship was tested and strained, he remained my friend until the day he died. As I thought about his gift of friendship, I remembered the last words I heard him speak. He was lying in his hospital bed following surgery, and he looked at Mike and me and said, "Thanks for coming. Thanks for caring."

Driving home with Kayla, I shared that story with her and told her about the final gift Geno had given me. Through his death, I found a sense of freedom. Geno had been my friend in good times and bad times. He had seen me at my worst and continued to be my friend. His death showed me I didn't need to try and meet the expectations of other people in order to have their friendship; I just needed to be me. People would either accept me and stick by me, as Geno did, or they would be part of my life for a short time for our mutual benefit and then we would both move on. For the first time, I was okay with that idea.

I will carry Geno's gift of friendship forever and walk into the future with renewed energy, a great sense of freedom, and excitement at the possibilities of the next steps along the path of my journey. Thanks, Geno. May you rest in peace. ∼

The Curse of Wide Ruins Trading Post

Janice M. Toland

"Don't go down there, it's *chindii*. It's cursed."

The voice came from the high side of the ravine called Wide Ruins Wash. Startled, I jumped and took a quick step back onto the roadway. On the heels of the statement came an amused laugh, as if the person talking was trying to scare me or perhaps wanted to make sure I understood they were too sophisticated to believe in curses.

Whoever it was had approached so quietly I hadn't even heard them, but the deep baritone voice let me know it was a male and from the choppy cadence of his speech I knew he was a Navajo. The amusement in his voice was especially irritating. I had spent the last week mustering the courage to climb down to the edge of the wash to pick through charred wood, twisted metal, and heavy stones. Now this buttinski was trying to stop me.

"Cursed? Why is it cursed?" I asked, looking up and shading my eyes against the bright Arizona sun with my hands. "Did a lightning strike cause the trading post to burn down?" I had lived on the reservation long enough to know traditional Navajos were extremely superstitious of anything that pointed, such as lightning, a knife, or an angry white teacher's index finger.

Ever since I had moved from Ganado to teach second grade at the Wide Ruins Indian School three months earlier, I had been curious about the pile of rubble strewn along the side of the wash. It was an eyesore beside the gravel road everyone used to get to the school and the houses for the teachers and staff. Once it had been an important trading post, famous for developing the beautiful and much-sought-after Wide Ruins hand-woven rugs.

"No, it wasn't lightning. People say the last trader burned the post down for the insurance money. It's the stones," he said, pursing his lips in the direction of the scattered rocks. "The stones are *chindii*."

My eyes had adjusted to the light enough to recognize the person who went with the voice. It was Phillip Chee, a young man who worked in the cafeteria kitchen. I had never spoken to him before, but I had noticed the ladies who worked on the serving line were always perkier when Phillip was around.

"Why would the stones be chindee?" I asked, trying my best to use the Navajo pronunciation for the word "curse." It crossed my mind that he could be making it up to see if I was gullible enough to fall for his story.

The image of the stoic stone-faced Indian does not apply to the Navajo people. They love to laugh and have a great appreciation for a good practical joke. Phillip Chee would no doubt find frightening a gullible white teacher extremely funny. Before long the entire community would know the new teacher might be book smart, but she was naïve enough to fall for a good prank.

"The first trader used the rocks from the houses of the Ancient Ones to build the original trading post and adjoining house. It's the stones. They're *chindii*," Phillip said.

"For God's sake, who would destroy an Anasazi ruin?"

"I just told you," he answered in the same teasing tone. He took a step forward, toward the edge of the wash, and then stopped. He hooked his thumbs in the front belt loops of his Wrangler jeans and gave me a brilliant smile. It was obvious he was well aware of his good looks and attractiveness to women. "The trader tore down the ruins."

"I know that's what you said, I'm not deaf," I snapped, "but isn't it against the law to desecrate ancient artifacts?"

"Now it is. If anyone tried something like that today they'd get arrested, but the first trader came here about 1900. Kin-teel had been sitting here empty for nearly a thousand years. I guess he figured there wasn't any need digging heavy stones out of the ground when the Anasazi had conveniently left him everything he needed just sitting there for the taking. It wasn't like they needed them anymore."

"Maybe so, but surely he must have known no traditional Navajo would ever go near anything touched by the Anasazi," I said.

"Oh, the trader had that covered. He knew a medicine man from over near Window Rock. The trader paid him to perform a ceremony that appeased the Anasazi and made it safe for the people to bring their wool and silver in to trade."

"So, why are the stones chindee now? If the medicine man performed the ceremony back then, isn't the appeasement still good?"

"I guess not. If the magic still worked, the trading post wouldn't have blown up when Bill and Sally Lippincott owned it," Phillip said.

I closed my eyes for a moment against the blinding sunlight, but I was also trying to wrap my brain around the notion that a medicine man's incantations could have a statute of limitations. Navajo beliefs may make perfect sense to them, but they were as confusing to me as they are to most outsiders. When I opened my eyes, Phillip was next to me. Just as I hadn't heard him come to the far side of the wash, I hadn't heard him move from the opposite bank to my side. I gave him a weak smile. The quietness of his movements unsettled me.

"What happened that time?" I asked, wondering what the odds were of a building being destroyed twice. Maybe the stones *were* cursed.

"It didn't burn the first time," Phillip said. After a pause he added, "It was more like . . . well, like it . . . exploded."

"Exploded? How does a trading post explode?" I didn't know much about the old Southwest trading business, but I knew the people from around Wide Ruins brought in rugs and jewelry, live sheep, and wool to trade for the things they needed, like coffee, flour, lard, and dried beans. It was hard to imagine how a business that dealt in things as harmless as sheep and turquoise could explode.

Phillip smiled at my obvious puzzled expression. "Old Joe Toddy blew the roof right off the building. That was way back.

Late thirties, maybe. When the Lippincotts owned the store, Joe Toddy was their handyman."

"Why would he do such a thing? Was he angry at the traders?"

"Oh, no, Joe was a gentle soul. He never would have done anything like that on purpose. He really liked working for the Lippincotts. He considered them friends as well as his employers. In his time of trouble, Sally closed the post and went with him to search for his older daughter after Mary ran away from St. Michael's Catholic Girls School. Joe never forgot that Sally had dropped everything to help him. He would have done anything for her."

"Well, if it wasn't on purpose, how did he manage to blow up the trading post?"

"Sally and Bill were having trouble with corn borers. The bugs got into the sacks of flour, sugar, and everything else. Out of desperation Sally sent away for some insecticide, this stuff called Wham. She'd heard about it on the radio. It was advertised as getting rid of any kind of bug.

"The Lippincotts were in San Francisco. Bill was giving a lecture on what it was like to run a trading post in the old Southwest. Just as he finished his talk he was handed a telegram saying the store had blown up."

I looked down at the remains of what had once been the heart of the Wide Ruins community. It was easier to imagine what it must have looked like after an explosion than to visualize it intact as an operating general store.

"The Lippincotts rushed back to find the roof had completely blown off and then dropped back on the walls of the store, except now the roof was sitting crooked. Everything inside the store was either blown to pieces or was sticking out from under the roof. At least Joe got rid of the corn borers. They blew out the top along with the rest of the contents of the store."

"I still don't understand how it exploded."

"Turned out the insecticide Sally sent for had a nitroglycerine base. Normally Joe didn't rush into things. He usually thought about what had to be done for a considerable amount of time before he actually got around to them. But Joe got carried away, and during the night, wham! There went the store." Phillip laughed as if the whole thing had been a huge joke on Joe.

Like every Navajo I had met, Phillip had inherited the gift of storytelling along with a wicked sense of humor. "What did Bill and Sally do?"

"Well, the first thing Bill did was spy his cowboy hat hanging off a splintered cornice. He grabbed it and plopped it on his head. It had survived the blast pretty much intact except for a hole burned through the back brim. After that, everyone called him Burnt Hat. He was still wearing the hat thirteen years later when he and Sally sold the store and moved to northern California."

"How do you know all this? It happened so long ago."

Phillip shrugged his broad shoulders. "It still makes a good story to tell around the campfire. Besides, Joe was what you *bilagaanas*, you white people, would call a colorful character. He was always getting into scrapes that were unintentionally funny.

"Navajos give everyone a nickname. We don't like people using our real names; they might wear it out. So everyone is called by a nickname. Bill was Burnt Hat, and Sally was called Red Hair for her long reddish-brown hair. If you stay here very long, you'll be given a nickname too."

"I can hardly wait," I said drily. Phillip chuckled.

"The Lippincotts had intended to remodel the store anyway. They didn't blame Joe. Once they finished, the store had all the modern conveniences. It had a level cement floor to replace the old flagstone and dirt floor, and glass counter tops and shelves replaced the old wooden ones. It even had a bubbling drinking fountain like those you see at the malls in Phoenix. Up until the renovations, there had just been a water pipe outside and everyone who traded at the store had to drink from the same dipper."

"Wow, sounds like they went all out. I bet everyone was impressed."

"Not exactly. Once the store was remodeled, suddenly they had no customers. No one would come near the store. Joe wouldn't go inside, and he worked there. The people believed that, for whatever reason, the Lippincotts had made the Ancient Ones angry, and that was why the store exploded. They were afraid the Anasazi would become angry at them if they came anywhere near the post and cause awful things to happen."

At that moment a truck came creeping over the hill and down toward the wash. The road was considered pretty good by Navajo standards, but the ruts and washboard bumps made even the worst rattle-trap pickup proceed with caution. The slow pace gave the dignified old Navajo woman, sitting backwards in the truck bed, plenty of time to get a good look at the new *bilagaana* teacher standing on the edge of the road beside a *chindii* ruin chatting with a Navajo man. She stared curiously until the pickup rounded the curve toward the boarding school and out of sight.

Phillip looked thoughtful for a moment and then said, "You've been asking a lot of questions. I have one for you. Why were you going down there? All the broken glass, twisted metal, and stones scattered everywhere, you should have known how easy it would be for you to get hurt."

"I don't know, just curious, I guess. Poking around an old trading post seemed sort of like a treasure hunt. I thought I might find something left from the old days worth collecting. I had no idea the place was cursed."

"I'd bet my silver rodeo buckle you don't believe in Navajo curses," Phillip said.

"It doesn't matter what I think. What's important is what the traditional people who live around Wide Ruins believe. I wouldn't want the parents of my students to be afraid to send them to school because of me."

"You could just hire a medicine man to get rid of the curse. That's what the Lippincotts did. They went to Joe for advice, and he recommended they hire a well-respected medicine man everyone called Loukaichukai. The day he came to do the ceremony, Joe went through the ritual with Bill and Sally and acted as translator. The Lippincotts were trying to learn Navajo but didn't understand enough to follow the directions of the medicine man.

"I don't know the prayers Loukaichukai said or the chants he used—it takes many years to learn to be a medicine man—but all Navajo ceremonies end with sacred corn pollen being thrown into the four corners of the building. After one last prayer the curse would have been removed, and the store was safe. Before long the customers began drifting back in to trade their goods for the things they needed."

"I don't know a medicine man," I said. "Besides, I understand they charge a lot of money if they have to get rid of a bad curse or perform a healing ceremony. I'm a teacher. I don't make much money. I probably couldn't afford a medicine man."

Phillip laughed. "Come on, I'll walk you home." He took my arm lightly to steer me away from the ruins back toward the school. "You could always pay the medicine man the way Loukaichukai asked to be paid for lifting the curse on the trading post."

"How was that?"

Phillip grinned. "Well, medicine men never leave the land between the sacred mountains, but they also need colored sand for their healing ceremonies. When Bill Lippincott tried to pay him, Loukaichukai said he had something else in mind. Loukaichukai wanted Bill to bring him an abalone shell, some black sand, and an ocean wave from his next trip to California."

"Oh, no, didn't he know that bringing an ocean wave would be impossible? He'd have to bring back a large section of the Pacific Ocean to Wide Ruins."

"That would have been quite a feat, but, on the other hand, it would be nice to ask the new teacher if she'd like to go surfing with me. What do you think?

"I think that sounds like fun. Except I'm from a landlocked state. I don't know how to surf.

"Then I guess we'd have to learn together. I can assure you, a desert-born Navajo doesn't have the slightest idea how to ride a wave either." ❧

Dying on Sandia Peak

Janice M. Toland

I knew I was going to die. I had never been more certain of anything. It suddenly seemed odd that I'd never given dying much thought before that moment, but now that I stared the Grim Reaper straight in the eye I felt paralyzed with fear. My heart pounded like the beat of a war drum, and my mouth felt so dry I could hardly swallow. All I could see from my vantage point were the tops of fir trees and jagged rocks hundreds of feet below where our bodies would be found bloody and broken.

My own death didn't bother me nearly as much as the thought of my mother and daughter losing their lives. For the first time in her life, my mother was ecstatically happy, madly in love with my stepfather and busy making plans for their retirement to Florida in a few months. Even more painful was the thought of losing my beautiful eleven-year-old daughter, just now showing hints of the independent and spirited woman she would become. My heart ached at the thought of her never becoming a teenager, never graduating from college, or raising children of her own.

My parents were living temporarily in New Mexico, and they invited Dawn and me out for a two-week visit. It was our first trip west of the Mississippi River and our first experience with a culture different from our own. For me, it was love at first sight. Albuquerque seemed so vibrant and alive compared to the stately antebellum homes and serene verandas of the south. Old Town Albuquerque turned out to be a charming plaza filled with colorful piñatas, baskets overflowing with flowers, and bunches of fiery red chilies hanging from covered sidewalks. Native American women sat on one side of the square beside brightly colored blankets covered with pottery, jewelry, and handmade baskets offered for sale.

A magnificent, three-hundred-year-old Catholic mission dominated the opposite side of the plaza with three-foot-thick, dull orange adobe walls and heavy cast iron bells formed by the hands of Native American slaves held captive by the Franciscan friars and Spanish conquistadors. In the center of the plaza sat an oversized three-tiered fountain surrounded by beds of showy flowers and small birds flitting about to drink or splash in the bubbling water.

A gentle breeze carried the heady aroma of spicy green chilies roasting over an open fire mingled with the delicious smell of tamales and burritos served in the many Mexican restaurants on the plaza's perimeter. The perfume of flower merged with the pungent scent of hand-tooled Mexican leather from the shops that sold belts, purses, and jackets. We heard music everywhere, from the lively Mexican mariachi to the soothing melodies of Native American flutes and the more energetic Navajo Yeibichai chants.

The glorious Sandia Mountains loomed over us on the eastern horizon, like the backdrop for a stage play. "Sandia" is the Spanish word for watermelon, and at sunset it's easy to see how the mountains got their name. The sun's low-light reflection transformed the mountains into a vivid shade of crimson, the color of the meat of a watermelon. The tall conifers along the ridge of the peaks shimmered a deep emerald, the color of the watermelon rind.

"There's supposed to be a restaurant at the top of the mountain," my mother said as we exited a leather shop.

"Really?" I answered, looking toward the mountains, already intrigued with the possibility of having dinner at the top. "How do you get up there? How do they get food up there?" I could see no scar to indicate a road.

"I'm not sure," Mother said. Since her statement had brought me to an abrupt halt, she stopped too. "I think there's a road on the backside somewhere. From this side of the mountain, I've been told there's a tram," she added with a resigned sigh. She knew my impulsive nature well enough to already regret ever mentioning it.

Growing up in the Mississippi flatlands, I'd never seen a tram. Well, not in real life. I'd seen one in a movie, a 007 that involved scenes of Bond hanging on to the cable for dear life as the tram plunged down the side of a snow-covered Alpine peak. I immediately disregarded that image. Such things only hap-penned in the movies. With the prospects of watching a famous New Mexico sunset while eating dinner perched on a mountain-top, my sense of adventure took over and I completely ignored any trepidation I might have had about riding up the side of a very high mountain in a small box swinging from a thin steel wire. As we walked to the car, I kept looking toward the moun-tains. "Wonder if you need a reservation to eat at the restaurant on top?"

"I guess we're about to find out," Mother said, giving me a long-suffering look.

We found a place to park and spent a few minutes doing what most vacationers do, taking pictures of ourselves with the Sandias in the background. We took pictures of the massive poles and cables that held the tram we could now see snaking down the mountainside. From the bottom with my feet standing secure-ly on the asphalt it looked innocent enough, but at thirty-three I was certainly old enough to know looks can often be deceiving.

The sun sank toward the horizon as we hurried to get in the short line to take the last tram run to the top. We planned to eat dinner, enjoy the view, look around a little while, and then take the last tram back down. Last up, last down. Once we climbed aboard, we discovered everyone had to stand during the ride. The car had plenty of room, so the three of us immediately went to stand by a window. The man who operated the tram suggested we might want to hold on to one of the poles that extended from floor to ceiling because the ride could get bumpy.

Bumpy? Just as the doors closed and locked, I decided I wasn't sure I liked the way he'd said the word "bumpy." Maybe this ride wasn't such a great idea after all. As usual with me, cau-tion came a little too late. The tram started with a jerk that had me grabbing for the pole, and in minutes we crossed over the first of the enormous poles that held up the cable. The tram shook like an old pickup speeding down a Mississippi back road as it crossed the connection, and I thought the whole thing would collapse. I spread my legs for balance, holding to the silver pole, and with my free hand grabbed my startled daughter. Lacking a third arm, Mother was left to fend for herself.

Within minutes we dangled hundreds of feet in the air, bumping over the support beams with the tops of trees below us getting farther and farther away. Mother and I exchanged a look over Dawn's head that said *What in God's name have we gotten ourselves into?* We weren't sure. The tram continued to chug skyward, and before long we couldn't see the trees at all from window. All around us we saw nothing but thin air.

Fifteen minutes and ten thousand feet later we got our first view of the platform where the tram would stop and dispose of its passengers. The small, wooden platform jutted out of the side of the mountain as if the builders, tired of working on the project, had hastily hammered it together without much planning or forethought. I'd seen hummingbird's nests that looked more substantial.

When we actually came alongside the platform, nothing about it changed my first impression. Two hefty guys stood waiting for us on the edge. Their job was to open the door, grab the door jamb, and hold it against the side of the platform so passengers could jump from the vehicle to the platform. Taking a deep breath, I jumped first and turned around immediately at the edge to catch Dawn. One of the guys told me to stand back. I gave him a withering look and told him to go to hell, that nothing on earth would keep me from catching my child when she jumped. She looked so frightened I don't think she could have jumped if I hadn't stood there with open arms.

Then it was my mother's turn. She told me to stand back, that she could do it better without my assistance. She leaped across the chasm with the grace of a ballerina. I shouldn't have been surprised; my mother moved through life with an ease and elegance I have never been able to achieve. Once all three of us stood safely on the closest thing to terra firma we'd experienced since we boarded the tram, I turned to look out over the precipice. It shocked me to see how high up we were. The Sandia tramway is the longest in the world, a fact that hit home immediately when my stomach churned and my knees almost buckled. By then the tram had taken on a load of passengers, the doors slammed shut, and it began a slow descent, snaking its way back toward the parking lot. Watching the little green-and-white car slowly pull away I knew that if this was the only way up to the peak, it had to also be the only way back down.

With a sense of resignation, I followed Mother and Dawn inside the building where we visited a small museum with old pictures showing the difficulty of constructing the Tramway and the strength of the cables. I found it mildly interesting, but the aroma of food drew me toward the restaurant. I turned to find my small, blond daughter rooted to a spot in front of the glass case holding a sample of the twisted steel cable used on the tramway. When I approached, she looked at me with huge blue eyes and in a terrified voice whispered, "We were hanging from that little wire, Mamma?"

"Well, yes, but it's there to show you that the steel cable is twisted for strength, to reassure you . . ." I stopped, knowing my words fell on ears that hadn't heard one word I had just said. I took her by the arm, steering her toward the restaurant. "It's perfectly safe. They wouldn't allow people to ride on it if it weren't." I wondered who I was trying to convince.

We sat near a huge window that overlooked Albuquerque and watched the sun dip toward the horizon in the distance as the lights of the city begin to twinkle on one by one far below. White billowing clouds formed on the western horizon, making the sunset even more spectacular. Mother remarked that it was like sitting in a landscape painting. We had no idea, sitting there watching as lightning flashed on the far horizon, that storms in the desert usually travel west to east and are both fast and violent.

Just as we got ready to pay our bill, the restaurant manager told us we needed to hurry. The approaching storm made riding the tram too treacherous for another run up the mountain to bring us down, so they were crowding everyone into the tram leaving in three minutes. We hastily paid our tab and rushed through the little museum. The force of the wind made it hard to open the door and all the people from the restaurant crowded the platform, lining up to wait their turn to board.

The temperature had dropped dramatically, and I hugged Dawn to me to protect her against the fierce, biting wind. A loud bang drew our attention away from the storm and toward the tram, the cable car slamming against the platform. The same two brawny guys holding the tram door had a hard time keeping it snug against the platform long enough for anyone to jump aboard. Between each person boarding they let the tram swing out and away from the platform, and when it swung back against the platform they would quickly grab the doors and the next person would jump. I had felt nervous on the ride up, but that trip would be a relaxing day at the spa in comparison to what the ride down would be like.

Dawn was eleven, almost too big for me to hold, but I wasn't about to let her try to time her jump so that she landed in the car and not fall hundreds of feet. When I picked her up one of the guys opened his mouth to speak and then recognized me as the one who'd told him to go to hell earlier. He didn't even protest my jumping with her in my arms. Dawn had her head buried in my shoulder, terrified. As they held the tram against the platform, I leaped inside. When we were safely aboard, Mother jumped next. We had made it past the first hurdle safely. From then on, getting down was completely out of our hands.

We waited while the rest of the passengers boarded, and then they closed and locked the doors. Banging against the platform one last time, the car pulled away from the crest of the mountain and began its slow descent. The wind swirled, and thunder crashed overhead as everyone hung on to the poles. It felt like trying to stay upright riding a pendulum. As the storm's wrath increased, we could again see the rocks and treetops far below. The storm reached the peak of its fury, and I felt convinced that we wouldn't make it to the bottom of the mountain intact. I could only visualize the car crashing with all the people aboard, including Mother, Dawn and me, falling to our deaths.

The little cable car kept chugging downward, and blessedly darkness fell so that we could no longer see the distance between us and the ground. At last the car made it to the bottom, and we all disembarked safely. I have often heard that people who survive a harrowing experience kiss the ground once they reach safety. I didn't actually bend down and kiss the asphalt of the Sandia Mountain Tramway parking lot, but I have to admit that it certainly crossed my mind. ∽

The Mystery of the Jerome Grand Hotel

Janice M. Toland

I've never been one to worry about things that go bump in the night. My practical mind just doesn't see any good reason for the spirits of those dead and gone to keep hanging around, bothering people and making a general nuisance of themselves. I always figured whatever business didn't get finished would just have to go undone forever once someone kicked the bucket.

I firmly believe there is no such thing as ghosts. Naturally (being the skeptic that I am) I'd wind up with a ten-year-old grandson whose favorite television show was *Ghost Adventures* and who, more than anything in the world, wanted to see a real ghost with his own eyes. That's how I found myself spending Halloween weekend at the Grand Hotel in Jerome, Arizona, with my daughter, Dawn, her older son, TJ, and Caden, the ghostbuster.

Jerome is one of several funky little towns scattered throughout Arizona that are fun to visit. The town hangs off the side of the mountain and looks as if the slightest breeze might cause the whole thing to go sliding the rest of the way down to the valley. In fact, back in the early part of the last century miners kept tunneling under the town to extract gold and copper until the entire town became unstable. The citizens of Jerome must have known something was wrong when their houses began slowly sinking or slipping off their foundations, and ominous cracks appeared in concrete walls and sidewalks.

One night the citizens of Jerome went to bed with the town jail on one side of the street, and during the night the ground shifted. When the residents awoke the next morning, the jail was sitting on the other side of the street. I've always wondered how the inmates must have felt locked inside a building that was slowing slithering down the mountainside. I imagine many prayers were sent heavenward from the prison that night with vows to stop drinking and promises to reform their wild and wooly ways.

Tombstone, probably the most famous of Arizona's funky little towns, was not the only dusty desert hamlet known for its rough and rugged habits. For a while people considered Jerome the wildest town in the territory. It had miners with money to spend, which naturally led to the standard fare of all Old West towns: brothels, saloons, gambling, and bar fights. Many of the injured wound up in the United Verde Hospital, a beautiful five-story Spanish mission-style building that sits at the peak of Cleopatra Hill, the highest point in Jerome, overlooking the town. It has a view to die for, literally and figuratively.

Luckily, the copper ran out and the miners abandoned the town before Jerome completely crumbled from the shockwaves of the mine blasts underneath. With the copper gone the miners moved away, and for years afterward Jerome was a ghost town. It sat forgotten as the homes of the miners and other buildings quietly decayed in the Arizona sun. Then, in the 1960s, hippies discovered Jerome and breathed new life into the once-dead town. The houses were cheap, the view from the mountainside was breathtaking, the climate was perfect, and, best of all, the ground had settled so that everything had stabilized and was again safe to live in. Today Jerome is known for its artistic shops selling paintings and pottery and its quaint bed-and-breakfasts and hotels. It's a perfect place for people who enjoy something a little out of the ordinary.

After sitting abandoned for forty-four years, the United Verde Hospital was bought and transformed into the Jerome Grand Hotel. The Grand is by far the most unusual place in a town where nothing is ordinary. Stories of the deaths of the miners, patients who suffered tuberculosis, and the inmates in the asylum are the stuff of legend. There was the caretaker who hanged himself in the boiler room, the handicapped man who rolled his wheelchair to the balcony railing and flung himself to his death, and the mining company executive who committed suicide by shooting himself in Room 32.

One of the best-known spectral residents was the hospital maintenance man, Claude Harvey. The hospital elevator fell on poor Claude's head back in 1935. Later the elevator was found to be working perfectly. What was Claude doing at the bottom of the shaft? Was he murdered? Was it a freak accident, or did he also commit suicide? The evidence is unclear, but hotel visitors claim to hear moaning, heavy breathing, and other strange noises emanate from the elevator shaft. Whatever happened to Claude Harvey, he seems to be the noisiest ghost at the Jerome Grand.

Everyone who worked at the hotel had a story to tell: footsteps in the hall when no one was there, doors opening or slamming by themselves, lights turning either off or on without warning. When we checked in, Caden could barely contain his excitement. He was totally convinced he'd have a paranormal experience while we were there.

This trip was what he wanted for his birthday. He told his mother he wanted to visit someplace that was haunted. He gave her a list of places he'd gotten from the Travel Channel's popular show. The list consisted of the Vulture Mine in Wickenburg, Arizona, the Winchester House in San Jose, California, The Stanley Hotel in Estes Park, Colorado, and the Jerome Grand Hotel.

His mom and I didn't exactly have the funds for an out-of-state trip and a mine seemed dirty and unappealing, so we chose the Jerome Grand through the process of elimination. We made reservations for the weekend of Halloween. What better time to go on the midnight ghost tour? We all hoped Caden would be granted his birthday wish and see a real ghost.

Sleeping in a hotel room that had once been a hospital is a little disconcerting. You are pretty sure people died in the room where you're sleeping, as well as in the room above and the one below you. We reserved a room on the fourth floor with double beds. Because of his age (ten), the hotel wouldn't allow Caden to stay on a floor with a balcony for safety reasons.

The original plan had been for the boys to sleep together and my daughter and me to sleep in the other bed. Once we had checked in, we squeezed ourselves and our luggage into the exact same elevator that fell on poor Claude Harvey's head. The elevator creaked and groaned with age while carrying us up to our room. An older couple rode up with us, and as the elevator chugged they began relating their experiences of seeing strange orbs of lights and waking suddenly to find a woman wearing a ghostly white gown standing at the foot of their bed. After that tale the boys decided to separate and each sleep with someone bigger than them.

Caden slept with his mother but was lying in bed facing me with a night stand between us. TJ, who was older, crawled in bed with me, put his oversized cold feet against my legs, and was sound asleep in seconds. Just as I was drifting off, I heard Caden whisper, "Nana, did you hear that noise?"

I opened one eye to see my younger grandson quickly scooting down under the covers and one small arm reaching up to grab a pillow to cover his head.

"No, Caden, I didn't hear anything. What do you think you heard?"

"I thought I heard someone say, 'Cla-ude Har-veyyy,'" a little voice whispered from deep under the sheets.

"Your imagination is running away with you. Stop thinking about Claude Harvey, and go to sleep," I said.

"Okay," he answered in a stage whisper, followed by a deep sigh.

Wasn't he the one who wanted to see a ghost? Now he was rolled up in a tight little ball as deep under the covers as he could get. I chuckled to myself and kicked at my older grandson to get his bony knees out of the middle of my back. How did I manage to wind up sleeping with the kid who is all elbows and knees?

When the room was finally quiet, I lay there listening. In a place like the Jerome Grand even a skeptic like me could lie in bed wondering if we were really alone in the dark. I didn't hear anything or see any strange lights and must have drifted off, because the next thing I knew the pale light of daybreak was streaming in from the windows. We had survived our first night without being awakened by a restless spirit.

After a day of shopping and sightseeing, which seemed to involve a lot of walking uphill, we returned to the hotel to get ready for our midnight tour of the parts of the hotel most likely to have paranormal visits. We were given an electromagnetic field (EMF) meter or an infrared (IR) thermometer and digital camera to help us locate and document the spirits, orbs, ghost sightings, and haunted happenings. Our tour began in the basement, and we were taken to the different floors and told the history of the hotel.

The third floor had been the surgery and seemed to me the creepiest part of the tour. The anesthesia available today was nonexistent during the early part of the last century. We stood where a century before people were operated on, babies were delivered, and bones were set with little or nothing to dull their pain. The toughness of those old pioneers, both men and women, amazed me. It was fun and interesting, but we weren't lucky enough to have a spectral visit us on the tour. Maybe my skepticism kept them away.

Then, wouldn't you know, my daughter was the one who had the paranormal experience. It was the day we were leaving, and she ran down alone to the check-out desk to ask about a nearby Mexican restaurant where we were considering having breakfast. She had questions about the quality of the food. While she was standing at the desk talking to the clerk, she heard someone drop something behind her. She thought someone must have come up behind her and dropped a heavy suitcase, waiting their turn to check in. She turned around, but no one was there. She turned back to the desk clerk, who was still raving about the food at the restaurant and interrupted him.

"Did you hear that?"

"What?" the clerk asked.

"Didn't you hear something heavy drop on the floor?"

"There's no one here but us, and I didn't hear anything," the clerk answered.

"But I didn't just hear it. I felt it. I could feel the vibrations under my foot exactly as if someone dropped something heavy," Dawn said.

"It was probably just Claude or the ghost of the old miner with the long beard," the clerk said. He paused and then shrugged. "These things happen here all the time"

Well, that was reassuring. Dawn was so unnerved she refused to get into the elevator by herself and made the clerk accompany her back to the room. We packed our things and checked out of the Jerome Grand. Caden was disappointed that it was his mother who had the paranormal experience and not him. TJ spent his time at the Grand bored out of his brain, because amusement parks are more to his taste than creaky old hotels. I left the hotel still firm in my belief that there really is no such thing as ghosts but also puzzled.

My daughter is level headed and a teacher; she isn't one for flights of fancy. When she showed up back at the room with the desk clerk in tow, I could tell she was truly unnerved. So, just in case I could be wrong about this whole paranormal business, as we bid goodbye to the Jerome Grand Hotel and backed out of the parking lot I said an old Scottish prayer:

> "From ghoulies and ghosties
> And long-leggedy beasties
> And things that go bump in the night,
> Good Lord, deliver us."

The Window Screen War

Janice M. Toland

I didn't fight in the window screen war. I was the innocent by-stander, sort of like the war correspondent who watches the action but tries to stay out of the fray. The war was over, of all things, window screens, but that just represented the surface battle. The real battle came in the form of a clash of cultures and for me, the observer, I received a lesson on how differently people see the world depending upon where they grew up and what their culture dictates is important.

I had accepted a position teaching second grade at Grease-wood Boarding School on the Navajo Reservation, working for the Bureau of Indian Affairs. When I signed my contract I had to raise my right hand and swear to defend the Constitution from all enemies both foreign and domestic. I hadn't expected to have to take an oath to teach seven-year-olds, and I began to choke up near the "So help me God" part. I would learn that when you teach for the BIA you need God's help and anyone else's you can muster.

The Navajo Reservation sprawls over 27,000 square miles of northeastern Arizona and spills into Utah and New Mexico. Greasewood, at the southern edge of the reservation, still managed to sit as far in the middle of nowhere as anyone could imagine. The closest grocery store was seventy-five miles away in Holbrook, Arizona, and visitors would find nothing in between except two trading posts, neither of which had a gas pump, and not much else except stunted pinion trees, nappy looking sheep, and an overabundance of mangy looking coyotes. The reservation offered an incredible wild beauty, but you had to stay there a while to appreciate it.

Norma and I met when we arrived at Greasewood to move into our houses and begin setting up our classrooms. That first day we were greeted by the office staff; the assistant principal, James Todd; the principal, Hubert Denny; and school secretary, Betty Yazzi. Mr. Todd escorted us into his office and unlocked a large wooden box that hung on the wall. Inside dozens of keys tagged with numbers hung on cup hooks. He chose two at random and handed one to Norma and the other to me. These were our house keys. That simple random act set the stage for a cultural conflict about the timeliness of when things should get done.

Greasewood had three short unnamed streets, the location of the houses of everyone who worked at the school. Evidently, whoever was in charge of building and painting the houses had one floor plan and two shades of paint. All the houses looked identical from the outside—stucco painted the exact same color as the dirt around them—to the interior—all painted the same shade of eggshell white. Well, they were all identical, except one. The house Norma got assigned had no window screens.

The second morning, Norma rang my doorbell so we could walk the short distance to the school together. When I opened the door she said, "All your windows have screens."

"Good morning to you too," I said, kicking a packing box full of dishes out of the way so she could get inside.

"Well, *my* house doesn't have screens," she said, putting her hands on her hips as if the assistant principal had deliberately given her a less-than-perfect house.

"I'm sure it'll be easy to fix," I answered, which only shows how naïve I was about trying to get anything done if you worked for a government agency.

As we walked to school she pointed out the window screens on all the other houses. It seemed every other house in Greasewood was blessed with screens, while Norma had gotten stuck with the one accursed house that had none.

"We'll see about this," Norma said. "I would like to raise my windows to enjoy the evening breeze, but I can't because none of my windows have screens."

As soon as we entered the school, Norma dashed into the principal's office to complain. I tagged along, grateful someone else was going to hear about her problem for a change.

"It's a simple fix," the principal said. "Mrs. Yazzi will give you the form. Fill it out and put it in the wire basket on her desk labeled Maintenance."

Norma got the required form, a half-sheet of paper in triplicate—white, yellow, and pink. At the top she wrote the date, her house number, and an explanation of her problem on the lines in the middle, signed it at the bottom, tore off the pink copy, and put the white and yellow copies in the little wire bas-ket. The pink copy acted as Norma's proof of when she'd put in the work order.

Then Norma turned to the secretary. "Do you have any idea when I'll get my screens installed?"

"It might be a while. This is a very busy time of year for the maintenance guys, getting the school ready. It's a lot of work." Betty Yazzi said. Then she added, "You could ask Mr. Leo Sangster. He's the boss over there."

Listening to the secretary, I imagined the guys from maintenance: tool belts hanging from their middles, bustling about climbing ladders to change fluorescent light bulbs, and slapping new coats of eggshell paint on dormitory walls. I had no idea that Navajos in general, and the Greasewood Maintenance Department in particular, had no concept of the word "bustle."

Navajos walk in beauty. It's a term heard frequently on the reservation. It means they strive to live in harmony with their environment and to achieve inner peace, which includes never getting upset or in a hurry. The Navajo language, one of the richest and most colorful of languages, doesn't even have a word for time. For hundreds of years their lives were governed by the cycle of the seasons, caring for pregnant ewes during the winter, shearing sheep and welcoming new lambs in the spring, following their sheep all summer as they grazed across an endless expanse of high desert, and gathering fire wood and pinion nuts in the fall. They understood their role in the grand scheme of things and had no need for a white man's clock. Over time I came to understand that even though Navajos live in what the outside world would consider abject poverty, they know more about living a contented life than we ever will.

Norma and I worked in our classrooms throughout the day, and as we headed home she decided that since we walked past the maintenance department anyway she'd stop in and inquire about her screens. We opened the door to the office, and the first thing we saw was a man sitting reared back in a wooden office chair, his scuffed western boots propped up on a large gray metal desk, his black cowboy hat pulled over his eyes. At one corner of his desk sat a wire basket with a handwritten sign that read, "Incoming mails," a testament to how difficult plurals can be when English is your second language. The basket was empty.

Scattered around the office were several other men either lounging on a sagging leather couch or sitting in straight chairs leaned back on two legs propped against the wall. They were all either dozing or talking softly in Navajo. After hearing the secretary explain how busy they were, I was rather surprised. It was possible we had interrupted their afternoon break, but I doubted it. I got the impression this was as industrious as the Greasewood maintenance department ever got.

Leo Sangster reluctantly took his feet off the desk, pushed back his hat, and gave us a sleepy look. He was middle-aged, his thick raven hair beginning to gray slightly at the temples. Rubbing his eyes, he asked Norma what he could do for her.

"I was wondering if you got my work order for window screens and when I could expect to get them installed," Norma said.

"No, we haven't gotten the work order yet. When we get it, I'll have to send one of the guys over to measure the windows. Then we have to order them from the warehouse in Gallup. If they have them in stock it shouldn't take more than a month. If they don't have them, they'll have to be ordered from the factory." He shrugged his shoulders as if to say, *Heaven only knows how long that might take.*

"Mr. Sangster, every house on the reservation was built using the same floor plan," Norma said, her voice rising in angry frustration. "You'd think they'd keep window screens in stock at the warehouse. Besides, why do you need someone to measure my windows? They're all identical. You could measure the windows at your own house,"

Leo Sangster's eyes narrowed slightly, a movement so tiny it was barely perceivable, but I knew Norma's anger had greatly offended the head of maintenance. I glanced toward the other men. They all sat stone-faced, staring into middle space. None so much as exchanged a glance, but I got the strange sensation that some sort of telecommunication took place among them in the glaring silence. I got the uncomfortable feeling their silent conversation didn't exactly compliment Norma or me. Navajos generally have great respect for teachers, but Norma's angry impatience proved she was out of harmony with nature and should be avoided. I didn't how we had offended them, but somehow I knew Norma wouldn't get her screens any time soon.

She began paying a weekly visit to Mr. Sangster in the belief that "the squeaky wheel gets the grease." On Friday we stopped by the maintenance office for the second time, and we lived through an exact replica of our previous visit. Leo's feet sat on his desk, the same men sitting on the couch and the same in the straight back chairs. There had to be some sort of pecking order that dictated who got the couch and who was relegated to the uncomfortable chairs.

"Any news on my screens?" Norma asked.

"No. We haven't picked up the work orders yet."

"It's been a week. You mean you haven't been over to the school all week? School starts a week from Tuesday."

"Joe was over there painting a classroom the other day, but he forgot to pick up the work orders," Leo said.

"You can see the school from your office window. How hard would it have been for him to turn around and go back?" Norma said.

"When Joe remembered the work orders, it was quitting time. The BIA won't allow us to work overtime."

A younger man, parked in one of the straight back chairs, nodded solemnly. He must have been Joe.

"That has to be the most useless bunch of men God ever created," Norma said once we got outside the door.

After Labor Day beautiful, black-eyed children moved into the dorm and school began. The work order finally landed on Leo's desk about the third week of school. He proudly showed it to Norma. Now he could take action, he assured her. Then the work order sat in the "Incoming mails" basket for several weeks.

Somewhere around the middle of October the weather changed. The Russian olive trees no longer permeated the night air with their exquisite perfume, and the leaves on the cotton-wood trees turned a brilliant yellow. The evenings became cool enough to need a jacket, and no one raised their windows. It didn't matter; Norma remained determined to push the mainte-nance men out of their inertia and force them install her screens.

She upped the ante by visiting the maintenance office every afternoon instead of once a week. If a squeaky wheel didn't get the grease, maybe an incredibly annoying wheel would do the job. By then everyone who worked at Greasewood School got sick of hearing about her screens. I suggested we take the screens off an empty house and put them on Norma's, but of course that was impossible. Something about certain screens being assigned to certain houses or some such nonsense.

By the middle of January, snow sat a foot deep and more than three feet deep around the eve of the houses where snow piled up after it melted enough to slide off the roof and then refroze. One bitterly cold day Joe showed up at Norma's classroom door. He said he was there to get her house key to measure her windows.

Norma nearly had a stroke standing at the blackboard. "Do you mean to tell me you haven't even ordered my screens yet?"

"No, I have to measure your windows first," Joe said. He looked younger than the other guys. I felt pretty sure he was the low man on the totem pole. He had to nap in one of the straight back chairs, and he got stuck with the thankless job of dealing with Norma.

As I settled into a quiet evening with a new romance novel, I heard a knock at my door. I opened it to find Norma standing on my stoop.

"Come with me. You have to see this."

I grabbed my coat, threw on my snow boots, and followed her over to her house. Instead of going inside she started around the corner toward the back. We had to be careful not to slip on the ice and snow piled up below the eve of her house.

Once we were at the back, she stopped. "What do you see?"

I didn't see anything unusual.

"Look again," she said, crossing her arms.

Then I noticed something in the pile of snow at the edge of her eves. It looked like writing. "What is it?" I asked.

"It's numbers. It's the measurement of my windows," Norma said. "Evidently, Joe forgot to bring a pad and pencil. He wrote the window measurements in the snow."

Then to my surprise she started laughing. "I give up," she said. "They win."

"Wonder if he'll be able to read them when he comes back?" I said.

"He won't be back," she said. "I'd bet my paycheck on it."

Spring came and baby lambs trailed behind their mothers as they nibbled yucca plants. The snow slowly disappeared and so did the measurements for Norma's screens. She raised the white flag of surrender and asked for a transfer, and I was glad I hadn't taken her up on the bet. The Greasewood maintenance department had won the war by simply digging in their heels and waiting.

In the 1600s George Savile said, "A man who is a master of patience is master of everything else." The Navajos know that better than anyone. ஒ

My Kind of Place

Rita Toma

As a native Canadian with retirement around the corner and grown children involved in their own careers, I only had to worry about myself. After three trips to Phoenix, Arizona, to visit my brother, John, I began dreaming of starting a new life. Someone once told me, "If you go to bed dreaming of what you want, the dream will happen."

It worked.

John needed an office manager, and I needed a job. Spring and summer are my favorite seasons, and where better to find these two seasons all year round than the Southwest? I love the sun, swimming, travel, and variety. I found the best combination of all my hobbies in Arizona.

Despite my resolution it wasn't an easy decision. My traditional side struggled with leaving a lifetime of family and friends, while my daring side said, "Just do it, and don't look back." Thanks to my parents I enjoy both Canadian and American citizenship, thus making my decision easier. So, at the young age of fifty-six, I decided to leave for an adventure.

I gave away most of my belongings, packed the truck with what was left of my Canadian memories (my brother, Tom, volunteered to drive it), kissed the kids goodbye, and wiped away my tears. On August 3, 2006, my sister, Karen, and I got into my car. Karen played navigator, and we spent the next three days driving south, away from Toronto, Ontario, Canada, to the Valley of the Sun.

What caused this hypnotic attraction? It wasn't just the weather, because Southwest summers can be stifling. Could it be the mountains I could see from every direction? My favorite mountains in Phoenix look like mounds of chocolate ice cream

186

covered with thick, dripping chocolate sauce, and John told me they're actually called the chocolate mountains. I later learned they were really called the Papago Mountains.

When I arrived my brother had bought a condo for me to rent. I always thought spending money on rent was a waste, so not long after I moved to Phoenix I began spending weekends with my realtor looking for an affordable, well-kept place in a safe area. We looked in Sun City, an active retirement community. At the time of purchase I didn't know what an active retirement community meant or how close I was to some of the most alluring places of interest.

One year almost to the day after I arrived in Phoenix I found myself unpacking again, this time in my new home in Sun City. When I looked out my back door the two large palm trees standing proud in the middle of my yard reminded me of one of the reasons I moved here. Palm trees scream "vacation," so it made sense to have them around to remind me that I now lived in permanent vacation mode.

On the winter weekends I picked oranges for my morning juice from my very own tree, a task that gave me a taste of sweetness and helped me start my morning with a smile. In Canada I would have had to buy oranges from the Ontario fruit stands or grocery stores, which didn't come close to walking out your back door. This experience of desert life confirmed my decision was the right move.

———◦◦◦———

Saguaro cactus is Arizona's proudest cactus. I have two defining my territory lines on the corners of my backyard. During its lifetime a saguaro can grow up to twenty-five arms on each cactus. Mine have several arms. If the arms could talk, each arm could tell their story of how the West grew during their time of growth.

As I walk in my neighborhood I look at the countless varieties of cacti with admiration and respect for their shapes and color. I look. I don't touch, for obvious reasons, but the spines on cacti don't keep me from loving Arizona landscaping. Most people, including back home in Canada, expect landscaping to mean grass and other greenery. Arizona landscaping replaces the grass with stones, which also means no lawn mowing—another plus point for moving to the Southwest.

Sun City functions as the best starting point for some exciting tourist attractions in Arizona. It didn't take me long to meet friends who enjoy the same desire to travel, another love to fulfill. We have spent weekends visiting the Grand Canyon, one of the wonders of the world, and also Sedona and Jerome, two of the most visited tourist attractions in the Southwest. Red mountains surround Sedona, making the city picturesque and cozy. Jerome's streets and homes need repair, but the leftover hippies are some of the most creative artists you will ever meet. The long hair, scruffy beards, and loose clothing take me back to my early twenties. The locals also boast of Jerome playing host to many ghosts, which both fascinates and intimidates me.

My friends and I frequent small towns for art festivals, rodeos, and various holiday activities. I enjoyed the art festivals and antique shops in small towns in Canada, but the Southwest offers a different flavor of talent. And who can give up a chance to go to Vegas? Four hours of driving, and I'm there. Sin City will always hold a spot in my heart and wallet.

I never get tired of one of my favorite sites that comes about thirty miles before you reach Las Vegas: the Hoover Dam, a man-made wonder of the world initiated by the 31st president, Herbert Hoover, and built as an agreement among nearby states for allocation of water. Ontario has Niagara Falls, a natural wonder of the world that draws crowds from everywhere. I marvel at this intersection of both my worlds and my love of travel.

Other amenities in addition to the charming landscaping attracted me to Sun City. On weeknights or weekends all year round, I can swim at any one of the seven available pools, all within a short drive or walking distance from my home. In my retirement community I can swim outdoors for eight months of the year, or longer if I wish, because all pools are heated during the colder months. After a quick set of laps or a run through the walking pool, I bask in the sun, living vicariously through the lives of the stories on my Kindle.

I call Phoenix winter months spring time, and I promised myself that I would start golfing when I retired. Now I live in an area renowned for its golf courses; people travel from all over the world to golf here. After several attempts to get it right, I realized that I would not become anything remotely close to what one would call a golfer. But I'm not a quitter. So I occasionally dust off my clubs and go for the free lessons offered by the retired pros. I should have guessed I was not a golfer when I asked how much lessons would cost and was told, "For you, thousands." Maybe I'm like a fine wine. I'll improve with age. I'm going with that one.

I joined the woodworking shop, although I really don't remember why. There's no better feeling than when you have made something with your own hands and can say, "I did that." Soon my children and siblings will feel obligated to accept handmade wooden crafts as gifts.

Along with all the activities I've enjoyed since moving here, I've also met dozens of new people. Snowbirds start to arrive in October and leave around the end of May. They double our population and come from other states and Canadian provinces. Yes, they too are running from the cold. With the snowbirds comes a geography and culture lesson. Each state differs from other states and the Canadian provinces. Instead of learning about cultures from Europe and Asia, as you would in larger cities in Canada, I learn very different interpretations of life from the Americans. My crystal ball predicts more travel by road in the near future.

My new life means more to me than just the active life of fun and learning new skills. It's about sharing my past and future with new friends. They welcome my stories instead of rolling their eyes because they've heard it before. Besides my brother and me, two more siblings have bought homes in the Southwest. Other family members have also discovered the Valley of the Sun, and each winter our homes fill with bodies yearning to get out of the cold.

Of course, I can't give Sun City a score of 100 percent.

Toronto traffic moves at the required speed, and everyone knows it's in their best interest to keep the flow of traffic. I have to fit my fun around my working hours, and time is of the essence. When I want to get some place quickly, the drivers in Sun City can definitely become a hindrance.

Some streets have speed limits of 25 or 30 miles an hour in order to accommodate golf carts, so naturally some drivers like to drive in the middle of the road at less than the required speed limit. But the golf cart drivers aren't the only offenders. Some people think they're out for a Sunday drive and stop in the middle of the road to admire their surroundings.

I used to be a good driver. Really. Now I dare you to drive in front of me while moving slower than the speed limit.

In these last seven years my immediate family tripled in size. My three children are married, and now I have seven grandchildren. I guess that makes it official: I'm of a certain age and belong in an active retirement area. So at Christmas I do the opposite of the snowbirds: I go north. I appreciate the snow and cold for a shorter period of time, knowing that I can escape to warmth.

I do love the stimulation and hustle of Toronto, a city with the same population as Phoenix but more condensed. I miss my children and grandchildren and know that when I finally—really—retire, I will spend more time with them. But right now I live in the best of both worlds. Soon I'll be at a time in my life where the only thing I need to do each day is decide what fun I will have, and some of that quality time will be spent in a quiet setting to satisfy another love: writing. The Southwest is the perfect place confirming my decision was right. It's my kind of place. ∾

Safe Is a Mirage

Rachel Wallis

Hoping for a hasty escape, I wheeled my suitcase down the hallway and into the elevator. The early hour made me expect a full descent, but the elevator stopped on the very next floor. My heart sank as the doors opened, because standing in the hallway looking like a page from a fashion magazine were my Texas cousins. They flitted on to the elevator like four colorful hummingbirds.

I couldn't believe my bad luck. I expected them to still be asleep, slathered in cold cream, hair wrapped in toilet paper; certainly not up, dressed to the hilt, rouged, shadowed, accessorized, and invading my elevator.

"Oh my goodness, where ya fixin' to go?" said Libby, the "baby" of the family—the smallest, the cutest, the blondest, and the one with the most 14K jewelry. Her pretty little face showed disappointment and concern.

"I have to get home," I replied. "I have clients waiting, contracts to write, and animals to feed."

"Oh, shoot! You can't leave! We got vistin' to do yet! Stay one more day. Please! We'll go shoppin' in town and have some supper."

"I'd love to, Libby, but I must get back. It's been so good to see all of you."

"Cantcha just stay and have breakfast with us?" Mary Ann wheedled. She was a few years older than Libby, just as pretty, slim, beautifully dressed, hair carefully coiffed, bejeweled, and so, so sweet. I just couldn't figure out why they irritated me so much.

"Gosh, I wish I could, but I promised my family I'd be back by noon and I have to get on the road." By this time the elevator had reached the lobby.

"Well, ya have to let me take a pichur for Patsy. She'll throw a hissy fit if I come back without a pichur of ya." Linda began to dig in her purse for her camera. "You girls line up over heah with Rachel now, and I'll get one of all of ya togetha."

They all obediently swarmed around me, and it dawned on me that I had on my most comfortable old jeans, a sloppy worn tee shirt, and no makeup.

*Dammit,*I thought, *why do you do this to yourself, Rachel?*

"Oh, wait! Libby you get over here and I'll take one of you and Rachel. Patsy will love that," said Clarice. "Bobby Jo, move over just a little. Now ya'll smile, ya heah? I'll swan, Linda, how do you operate this camera? Oh, nevah mind, I got it. Don't move! Everybody, smile now . . . smile Rachel . . . come on now, give me a smile, sugah."

Forty years of competing with the Washburn cousins should have prepared me better than to get caught at 6 A.M. sneaking out of the hotel to avoid goodbyes. Patsy was a high school rival and was now Libby's best friend. I could just imagine them smiling knowingly at each other over the picture of poor old Rachel who had always been rather plain but had now completely gone to the dogs in the beauty department. How the heck would I get out of this gracefully?

No way, you idiot, I raged secretly at myself. *Just act like you're having the time of your life, and try to be nice.*

So we posed for pictures, me in my frumps, the Washburn sisters in their breakfast finery.

That should be a treasure for the family album, I groused silently.

After what seemed like a lifetime of small talk, promises to call, assurances that I would come to the next family reunion at "Bobby Jo's place in Dallas," and lots of hugs and kisses, I finally escaped with my suitcase and hurried to my car. I tossed it in the trunk of the big gray Cadillac with a force that bore witness to my irritation and headed east on W. Casino Drive looking for Highway 163, which crosses over the Colorado River from Laughlin,

Nevada, into Arizona. Then I picked up Arizona 68 toward Kingman, slipping in a CD. Soon the voice of Alfred Molina reading Larry McMurtry's *Sin Killer* emerged from the Bose speakers and surrounded me with calming sound that I could give my full attention or just tune out and let my thoughts wander.

The Cadillac wasn't new. I had bought it at an intensely negotiated price from a private owner in Sun City with only 42,000 miles on it. The big, comfortable vehicle offered a controlled climate and was conservative enough to be respectable. The gray leather seats gave it the look of luxury that impressed my home-buying clients. It was a prized possession and a needed tool in my business, therefore a luxury that I could justify in my own mind.

I merged onto Interstate 40 at Kingman. A little more than 20 miles east of there, Arizona Highway 93 veers southeast toward Phoenix and traverses the transition of the Mojave Desert to the Sonoran Desert.

Always interested in developing areas of real estate, the few small ranchos starting to populate the area intrigued me. The Hualapai Mountains sit just to the west, the Buckskin Mountains lie off in the hazy blue-gray distance, and farther away, fading into the skyline, are the Rawhides. Distances seem greater here under the cloudless sky, objects seem smaller, and I felt an eerie aloneness. There even seemed to be a lack of traffic on the highway.

The foothills are covered with creosote bushes, prickly pear, cholla, night blooming cereus, palo verde trees, ocotillos, mesquite, and huge saguaro. I marveled at the centuries-old cacti with their numerous little holes carved by wood peckers. These tiny holes become homes for small animals, owls, finches, sparrows, and marlins, converting the huge old cacti to sky-condos-with-a-view for desert creatures.

I had read that the ironwood, palo verde, and mesquite are often "nurse trees" for the saguaro, providing a safe place for the seed to hide, sometimes for years, before it takes root and starts to grow. Because of its slow growth—a total of 1 to 1½ inches the

Rachel Wallis

first 8 years—it often outlives the host tree. Thus the pale green palo verde, the grayish green ironwood, and the darker, richer green of the mesquite dot the landscape around the saguaro, as the brush of an impressionist artist applies color to the canvas.

I regressed to my childhood, remembering the days when my sister and I hung out the back window of the car and searched the distance for a mirage. Sure enough, I saw one down the highway ahead of me flashing on and off in the desert sun, urging the traveler on with its promise of solace.

As I approached Wikieup hunger overtook me, so I decided to stop for a brief breakfast of huevos rancheros and coffee at a place about three miles out of town. The café was deserted except for a small, neat Mexican lady who took my order, cooked my meal, and carefully placed the steaming hot dish in front of me. She was busy watching a TV in the kitchen and only came out once to refill my coffee cup. I had no complaint; the food was great, the price was fair, and the solitude of my tiny table was preferable to the busier Wikieup Trading Post. I sat there and reflected on the humiliation of my early morning encounter with my cousins, licked my wounds a little, and then I paid and left.

Highway 93, also known as Joshua Tree Forest Parkway, cuts right through one of the few areas in Arizona where you will find the Joshua tree. I passed the Big Sandy River, dry as a bone on this beautiful morning. Here the cliffs started to rise sharply on each side, and huge rocks, piled one on top of the other like hoodoos, surrounded the saguaro. A sign pointed to the left to the tiny old town of Nothing, and I resisted turning down that road to explore what looked like from the distance a huge pile of junk.

Soon the Joshua trees started to come into sight. First a gigantic one right beside the road that looked like something you might find in a Dr. Seuss book, then more and more until I was surrounded on all sides by the gnarly old trees growing happily alongside the saguaro. A highway sign declared "Joshua Tree Parkway of Arizona." These caricatures are not even trees but yuccas that are members of the lily family, and they do actually bloom a beautiful white flower from March to May. But for the rest of the year their grotesque bent arms and legs, with bunches of long spike-like thorns and sharp green leaves bristling at the ends, inspire visions of Indian ghost dancers with feathered headdresses. I imagined the ghosts—high on peyote—dancing across the creosote carpeted foothills.

The beauty of the desert was all around me as the Northstar engine hummed and the chrome spoke wheels ravished the road. Even though it was September and the desert had just survived the summer temperatures hotter than 110 degrees, the colors and textures of the landscape combined to soothe and please the human spirit. The purple mountains in the distance, the red rocks of the foothills and hoodoos, the myriad of colors and shapes of the cacti, trees, and bushes provide a unique sight-seeing experience.

Soon I was turning left in the quaint Western town of Wickenburg. Here huge old cottonwood and willow trees follow the Hassayampa River, making a luxuriant oasis in stark contrast to the desert I had just left. I took the route that crosses the bridge onto Highway 60, and it was just a short drive from there to my home in Glendale.

No one else in the family was home that day, so I carried my suitcase in and started to unpack and put my things away. The first person I called was my friend, Linda, who had stood in for me, answering my calls, handling my files, and executing any paperwork that couldn't wait for my return.

"Hey, Linda, I'm back. What's up?"

"Rachel? Geez, kiddo, how was the reunion? Have a good time?"

"It was good, and I saw a lot of people I hadn't seen in years. We're all getting old. Thanks loads for taking over for me. What's going on?" I asked.

"Well, just all this stuff back east. That's all anybody can think about right now."

"What do you mean?"

"Well, you know, the World Trade Center," she replied.

"The World Trade Center . . .? What are you talking about, girl?"

"Don't you know? How could you not know? We've been attacked. They've flown a plane into the Twin Towers in New York City and another into the Pentagon. Also, a plane has gone down somewhere in Pennsylvania. Turn on your TV, Rachel. Oh my goodness, I can't believe you don't know about it. Didn't you have your radio on in your car?"

"No, I was listening to a book. You know me! That's how I travel," I reminded her.

"You're probably the only person in the United States who doesn't know what's going on. Put your TV on Channel 12 and you'll hear all about it. They're still not sure it's over; there may be more attacks. All airports are closed. Your files are fine. We'll talk later. I've got to watch this." And she was gone.

All airports closed? I thought of my Texas relatives stranded in Laughlin with no flight back to Dallas. Would they have to rent a car and drive all the way to Texas? Irritating or not, they were my family and I felt concern for their safety. I also felt a little bit guilty. They weren't that irritating! I could have been nicer. What if something terrible had happened and I never saw them again? I vowed to contact them as soon as possible. Maybe attend next year at Bobby Jo's place.

The shock of it all had not sunk in yet as I walked over and clicked on the TV. As I flipped through the channels, I found the news reports everywhere. Over and over the planes flew into the towers and the whole thing imploded.

I was horrified. Alone, I sat down and cried. I'm not sure how long I was there, but as I watched I learned that while I was still dressing that morning American Airlines Flight 11 had flown into the North Tower. People were already dying while we were riding down in the elevator. Oblivious to what was going on in New York City, I had been focused on my escape from the reunion and posing for photos in the lobby while United Flight 175 had flown into the South Tower. While I had been leaving Laughlin first the South Tower and, 30 minutes later, the North Tower had collapsed, killing 2753 of our countrymen.

Safe in the cocoon of the big gray car speeding down the

scenic route to the safety of my home, I had no inkling of the experiences of the people watching it unfold on radar screens, of military jets being deployed, of panicked air traffic controllers trying to make sense of garbled messages from hijacked American Flight 77 as it flew into the Pentagon. Then, while leisurely eating my breakfast in Wikieup, people just like me who had boarded United Airlines Flight 93 in Newark and had expected to go home to their families that night were flown to their death in a lonely field in Pennsylvania.

Had the God of the universe been watching over me when I arose so early and left the hotel, when I popped that CD into the stereo, breakfasted alone at the deserted café?

All morning I had treasured the beautiful countryside in solitude, free to take in the beauty around me, while chaos had ripped through our country and destroyed almost 3,000 of our countrymen on a day that would forever be known as 9/11.

Gratitude washed over me that fate had given me a short reprieve and granted me my own personal few hours of innocence and safety. ❧

You Asked About My First Love

Rachel Wallis

The summer of 1953 Dwight Eisenhower was our president. The "I LIKE IKE" sticker adorned every vehicle we had, and Daddy sat by the radio at night and cheered Ike on. The rest of the family loved Ike too, because we listened to Daddy curse Roosevelt and Truman all through the war years and our ears appreciated the silence.

Daddy insisted on morals. He kept a bottle of Hill & Hill whiskey for coughs, but no one in our family dared to swear, smoke, play pool, or gamble. However, when it came to presidents, Daddy could think of more curse words than just about anybody in New Mexico.

I had just turned twelve the prior spring and, because I had skipped a grade, looked forward to high school in the fall. Bear in mind that back then twelve-year-old girls in the country matured early. My first date had been a bit of a disaster with Daddy following right behind in his car, but it qualified. I had been kissed quite thoroughly, although secretly, and felt genuine gratitude toward the young man responsible. He had risked facing Daddy's huge old Colt 45 to assist me in achieving my first-kiss status.

My nearest sister, Patty, seven years older than me, married that year, leaving me alone at home with my aging parents. We lived on a ranch 10 miles outside of a small town that barely qualified as a wide spot in the road, on Highway 66 between Albuquerque, New Mexico, and Amarillo, Texas. We were dryland farmers and mother cow ranchers on unyielding land that Daddy had bought in the early '40s for a few bucks an acre. I rarely saw a person except for school, so summers dragged by and loneliness remained my constant companion.

Patty married a tall, good-looking Texas cowboy named Dale, and he had five brothers (Darrell, Brett, Harold, Calvin, and Jarod) and four sisters (Sis, Bernadine, Maxine, and Sue.) Ten children in all. I met Darrell right away because he worked with Dale, and I eventually met Harold, Calvin, and Jarod when they came to visit. Mama said they were all a little Texas Panhandle backward because they were so shy.

Then one summer day Patty and Dale's car pulled up, and out stepped this tall, sun-tanned, uniformed, dark-haired man with the bluest eyes I had ever seen. When they introduced me to him, he ducked his head, looked up at me under long dark lashes, and flashed a shy smile. Oh, my God! Here was the handsomest man in the world, and he was standing in my own front yard.

"We brought the ice cream freezer, fresh peaches, and plenty of ice," said Patty. "Brett hasn't tasted homemade ice cream in two years, and he's ready to turn the crank if you're ready to sit on the freezer."

I grinned and managed to whisper, "Okay."

"Well, then, come on and help me get it mixed up."

I felt relieved to be away from the men. I shook, and my knees felt as if they might give way. I wanted to glance back and see if he was watching as I followed her into the house. I didn't dare mention to Patty that I had already fallen crazy in love with her brother-in-law for fear she would tease me about it and make me look foolish. I just acted real cool and thanked the Lord I had on my best pair of Levis and the cute white piqué top that showed my sun-tanned shoulders.

"Okay," Patty called out to the men, "you guys better get in here. We've got the ice cream in the freezer. Now it's all yours to freeze." With that Dale, Brett, and Daddy brought in the ice and packed it in the freezer, salted it down, and placed a folded towel on top so that I could sit on it to keep it steady while they took turns at the crank.

I sat very still and said nothing. My heart pounded, and my face felt all moist and warm. Occasionally I would glance at Brett, and he would flash me another one of those heartbreaking smiles. We never said one word to each other all night, and when he left I didn't see him again for a long time.

He went back to finish his enlistment in the army and I continued being a lonely young girl on a remote ranch going to high school in a small town. I studied, listened to Lefty Frazell, Johnny Cash, and Hank Williams, read True Romance, daydreamed, and thought of the things I would like to say to Brett. I developed into a woman, and I studied my pretty, young, bare body in the mirror and tried to imagine what he would think if he could see me like that. I read somewhere about telepathy, so I lay in my bed long into the night, sending my thoughts across the miles with all my mental might, praying that he was receiving them at the other end, hoping that he would somehow know how much I loved him, and love me in return.

Patty and Dale moved into the old Parr place up on the hill about three miles from us. One day she said, "Guess what? Brett's coming home, and he's going to take over Dale's old job and live with Darrell at the Griffin ranch." She grinned. "If you're a good girl maybe I'll invite him over, and you'll get to sit on the freezer again."

I did see him a few times. Not as often as I longed for, and the situation never lent itself to conversation. I think my sister enjoyed being the center of attention with the three big cowboys, and neither she nor Dale wanted to risk Daddy's ire by putting me in the company of an older man. Brett occasionally came to our home to help us brand our cattle, and I watched in awe from a distance.

He went his way, and I went mine. I dated steadily and had boyfriends my own age. It didn't keep me from loving Brett, though, and thinking of him constantly. I heard through Patty that he was carousing with an older woman who had been married, divorced, and had children.

Then one night our school had a Halloween carnival, and I had been chosen carnival queen. My friends and I had set up a booth with a bean bag toss and stuffed toys as prizes with one huge teddy bear for the grand prize. Imagine who should walk in—Brett! He had been to the bar and had had a few, so he was not at all shy and he stalked right on over to my booth and start-ed flirting. I was a little more self-confident by then, so I flirted right back and he stuck around and won the big teddy bear.

"I'm going to give this to you," he said. "But I really think I should get a kiss from the queen of the carnival."

My friends pushed me toward him and I shyly kissed him on the cheek. I'd never kissed anybody in front of witnesses, and I knew if Daddy found out about this I was in big trouble. It seemed as if all my dreams had come true in one night. Brett took me next door for refreshments, and as we walked through the big gymnasium with all my friends watching, he took my hand, tucked it inside his arm, and smiled down at me as if we alone shared a wonderful secret. We sat and talked about our families for a while, but when we strolled back to the booth I saw the gal he had been dating: older, wiser, much more available. She took hold of his arm and dragged him away. I was crushed, but I still had my teddy bear as living proof that we had been together.

Not long after that my brother had a dance at his house, and my best friend and I got it into our heads to drive down to the ranch and invite Darrell and Brett. They must have seen us com-ing for miles away, because Daddy's '56 Chevy pickup kicked up a huge cloud of dust on the 15 miles of dirt road. To our surprise they agreed, so we spent the next week preparing and giggling.

I made myself a pretty blue cotton-satin dress. It had an empire waist with a peasant style top, and the elasticized neck could be worn either just plain round or you could pull it down on the shoulders. From the empire waist down it was princess style so that it fit my waist and then flared out over the full pet-ticoats that we wore in those days. I was sweet sixteen and prob-ably at the very best that I would ever be, but still young for a twenty-eight-year-old man.

When they walked in, they took off their hats. My brother went over and greeted them, and then everyone else continued to dance and have a good time. They just stood there inside the door holding their hats, and nobody said a word to them. It was one of those horribly awkward situations no one seemed to be able to correct. Betty and I hoped they would come over and ask us to dance, but they never did. Out of respect for our family they had denied themselves the few drinks it took to loosen up, and they were just too shy to make a move. Finally they put their hats on and walked out. We jumped into action and ran after them.

The only thing I could think of to say was, "Y'all come back now," and they actually turned around and started back in the house. I just couldn't face more embarrassment. I thought if they walked back in that house again I would just drop dead, so I blurted, "No, no, not now!" They halted again and turned back to leave. We mustered the good sense to thank them for coming and chat with them for a few minutes, and when they were gone we collapsed, laughing, on the lawn.

I wrote off any possibility of a romance with Brett after that. I figured he thought of me as that stupid little nut-case who invited him to a party and didn't have the sense to know how to act once he got there. One night I passed the bar next to the movie theatre, glanced through the open door, and saw him inside all liquored up and dancing with the owner's wife. Anger, disgust, and perhaps jealousy rose inside me. My naiveté revolted at the idea that my handsome, bigger-than-life cowboy was there in front of me dog drunk and sweaty, dancing with tacky old Mrs. Boggs. Tears scalded my cheeks all the way home.

I told myself for a long time that I hated him. Not long after that I married at the ripe old age of seventeen, in spite of Mama and Daddy's protests. The quick romance turned into a ten-year disaster. Soon after that, Brett married the older woman with four children, and five years later we wound up living in the same town. His wife was Jehovah's Witness, so he became a preacher and went door to door proselytizing to please her. I started frequenting the bars with my husband, trying to drown my unhappiness in booze and dancing. What a switch! Occasionally I saw him at some café with his wife and spoke to them. He would jump to his feet and act friendly but his wife always acted snotty, so I figured she suspected I still carried a torch.

I went through a divorce and a torrid romance with another man that left me seeking solace in things familiar and gentle. I wanted so much to call Brett but, of course, I couldn't. He was married and had all those little boys.

Then I met Don and we married. A good marriage but, as all good marriages do, it had its moments. I still thought of Brett occasionally. We moved far away, and when I called my sister I pumped her for information about him. My niece was grown and she loved to hear the story about her Uncle Brett and me. We all laughed and joked in secret about the big love of my life and how, if his wife died, I would appear at the right time and grab him. It even got to the point that I would call my sister when I was depressed about something and open our conversation with "Is she dead yet?" It was just a silly joke, although cruel, a girl thing between sisters. But his wife lived, and we all aged and passed the point of romance.

Many years passed before I saw him again. In 2004 my wonderful brother-in-law passed away, and I flew home to attend his funeral. There were all those tall, good-looking brothers and their wives. We hugged and comforted each other, and then Brett and his wife walked into the room. I once had the privilege of meeting movie star Randolph Scott in person, and I swear Brett looked just like him. He stood tall, slim, and erect in the same military way, with graying hair and those clear blue eyes.

I waited until the right moment and walked over and spoke to his wife and then turned and offered him my hand. He took it and for just a moment he started to shake it. Then he smiled and pulled me into his arms for a wonderful long hug and kissed me on the cheek.

His wife looked as if she might fulfill my fantasies and croak on the spot. My sister just looked surprised and a little dazed. But my niece had a huge smile on her face, and my heart raced just like it had the first time I saw him. All during the day, every time I looked his way, he flashed the same heartbreaking smile. Sixteen was gone forever, but I felt delighted, radiant, and yet at peace, because I realized that he, too, remembered the sweetness of the few moments we had shared.

There are many kinds of love, but innocent first love, reciprocated or not, is hard to beat, because of its purity, and even harder to forget. A love that does not have to stand the test of marriage, finances, children, broken promises, arguments, and stinky laundry can be treasured for a lifetime. ∽

Follow the Sun

Dori Williams

June 2004

The buzz of the circular saw rang in my ears, a deafening sound I had become very familiar with. My husband, Bob, cut a piece of trim to frame the window of our Victorian house. I had started this renovation project twelve years earlier, long before I had met him, when I was single.

I did a lot of the work myself to save money. I became a ceramic tile prodigy. I plastered walls to give them that old-world charm, painted, and wallpapered. I stripped a hundred-and-fifty years of paint off of every piece of trim and door in the house and brought them back to their natural beauty. But now the project had become a joint labor of love.

Bob stood on the ladder. I handed him the piece of trim and watched him carefully nail the aged piece of oak into place. I smiled, and my heart filled with love for this man who had become such an important part of my life. The energy and love that we drew from each other grew deeper and richer with each passing year.

I watched as he cut the next piece, my eyes transfixed on the spinning circle of steel. The circle had no beginning or end. The constant perpetual motion transformed everything it pulled into its energy.

The universe works the same way. Energy is spinning within the circle of life. We are energy in a constant state of transition, and energy doesn't die. Our energy is transformed. The spinning circle always returns to its original point. If life is a circle, then physical death is only the birth to a new existence. Life is eternal.

I stood there mesmerized, contemplating the deeper meaning of life, watching the blade whirl at warp speed like the passage of time.

Dori Williams

January 2000

It was a new millennium, and the world had not come to an end as some predicted. Instead, I sat at a table in a hotel in Milwaukee, Wisconsin, tapping my foot to the beat of the music. A large wooden dance floor encompassed the center of the room. The dimmed lights enhanced the light show that ricocheted off the mirrored ball spinning droplets of color around the room.

I met a man that night. A mutual friend had told him about me and our common interest in house renovation and remodeling, and on that cold crisp night in January at a dance I met my husband.

My future husband smiled, stuck out his hand, and said, "Hi, my name is Bob. I understand that you can swing a mean hammer."

I took his hand and smiled back.

"You better believe it, and I can plaster with the best of them."

We both chuckled and conversed for a while, and then he asked me to dance. Little did I know that night that those spins around the dance floor would symbolize the start of my journey on this circle of life with my husband, spinning us in the direction to follow the sun.

My husband had a desire to go back to school and become a doctor. It was a lifelong dream of his. I admired his aspirations and made him an offer he didn't refuse.

"Why don't you move down with me? There's a university not far from my house."

It was a win-win for both of us, and it gave us the opportunity to be together. He dove into his studies for three years. I even helped him by writing some of his papers. And when an occasional remodeling project came up, he'd help me. His dream and goals now became mine. I dedicated the next fourteen years of my life to helping his aspirations become a reality and waited patiently to reap the benefits of years of sacrifice, to move somewhere warm so our families could share in our dream when they came to visit.

Then the realization set in: he was forty-four, he still had to get through years of medical school and residency, and he had accumulating debt and would be out of the workforce for a long time. So Bob switched majors. He obtained a four-year nursing degree, a BSN, with a minor in biology and graduated cum laude in 2008. Not too bad for an old guy.

During those tough years we pulled together and made it through. But once he graduated we wanted to leave the snow and ice in Wisconsin behind.

October 2008

After graduation Bob decided to explore re-entering the army. With his six years of prior military experience it put him on the cusp, age-wise, to be able to re-enlist as an officer. If he could re-enlist, the listing bonus would pay for most of the school loans.

The recruiter sounded encouraging. However, Bob had some medical issues he had to get cleared first. The recruiter was confident if Bob were cleared medically, his age wouldn't be a problem.

The paperwork began; I had to contact numerous agencies to get all his past military records, which took constant follow up. Then the waiting began. The army flew Bob out to Fort Sam Houston to the hospital in San Antonio, Texas, for an interview and physical. All went well; we felt encouraged. But then January, February, and March went by, and we received no word about his medical clearance.

"We really are in need of good medical help," the recruiter reassured us.

I was excited about being an army wife. As soon as we got the clearance we would get married so I could travel with him and start our new life adventure. He had asked me to marry him on Valentine's Day 2001, but we had put our wedding plans hold until he finished school. But every day brought us closer to the reality of the dream we were building.

April 2009

Finally, Sergeant Yaser called and gave us the news.

"It looks like everything is cleared out in D.C. Make your

wedding plans, and when you return from your honeymoon we will enlist you."

May 9, 2009

Our friends have a home in Estrella Mountain Ranch in Goodyear, Arizona. They graciously hosted the wedding in their lovely yard. It was decorated with tiny white lights around the garden, and the flowers were in bloom. Their yard looked over the lake, and the mountains provided an aesthetic backdrop.

I slipped the gold band on Bob's finger. The circle of the ring in the marriage ceremony is a symbol of continuity and infinite love. It reminded me of our unending love and how our energies became connected and part of the greater circle of life. We enjoyed our sunset ceremony with family and friends and we danced to the song, "Grow Old with Me." And I was expecting the best was yet to be. It was a happy day.

During our honeymoon our minds and thoughts whirled with excitement and anticipation at Bob's reenlistment. But when we returned home another phone call from Sergeant Yaser quickly extinguished that excitement.

"I have some bad news. I am not going to be able to enlist you like I thought. With the downturn in the economy we are getting a higher influx of younger people enlisting, and the army has more applicants to choose from now. But I am going to give you the names of some people to contact and see if we can get this denial overturned."

We tried to get it overturned to no avail for several months. What once was a hopeful proposition turned into a lost cause. We set our course in a new direction: Phoenix.

June 2009

We still wanted warm weather and we had friends in Arizona, so that seemed like a logical place to start. It made sense for Bob to try to get a federal job so his past military experience could be applied to his retirement. So I became his official secretary. I spit-shined his resume and sent it through the USA jobs website to every job offer that he might qualify for and also sent his resumes directly to government agencies. Applying for government jobs requires extra documentation, and I mailed, faxed, or emailed packages of twenty or more pages. I turned down a job to make this my full-time effort. I sent out hundreds of packets during the next six months to Arizona, California, Texas, Florida, North and South Carolina, Louisiana, and New Mexico.

I searched every state with a heat index above freezing in January. By September we even looked back to Wisconsin in desperation for work. So many factors worked against Bob: his age, being a new grad, the worsening economy, and the job market drying up. Had he just invested the last eight years of his life, gone into debt up to his eyeballs, and put our lives on hold to be unemployed?

November 2009

Finally Indian Health in Phoenix took the bait. Phoenix: just where we wanted to be. We were excited and then realized the catch. Their main office was in Phoenix, but the job offer was at a hospital in Whiteriver, Arizona, about three hours north of Phoenix on an Apache Indian reservation. My naiveté immediately conjured visions of tepees and the "Wild West."

Okay, the location wasn't ideal. But we were desperate, so he accepted the offer. I rationalized that anything in Arizona had to be pretty warm in the winter, right?

After some research I found out that we would be at an elevation of about 6,000 feet, and, yes, we would be looking at snow once again.

December 2009

My husband moved first. I finished up our affairs in Wisconsin and followed about a year later with a couple of lengthy visits in between. I had three floors of a house, a basement, and a garage and eighteen years of stuff I had to deal with, pack, or throw out. Our belongings were moved across the country into a modular home in a small subdivision behind the hospital with other doctors and nurses.

The cool mountain air, crystal-clear lakes and streams, and the rich Indian culture were inviting and interesting. And trees. Lots of trees. A large stand of ponderosa pines graced this area of northeastern Arizona known as the White Mountains.

It also made it a tinderbox for wild fires.

Summer 2011

A fire broke out and spread rapidly. Officials evacuated the hospital, and we left our home with whatever we could jam into the car, including our dogs, Dolce and Gabbana. We stood in our backyard and watched the devilish red inferno creep closer to our home and wondered if the fire would devour all of our worldly possessions. I watched the planes circle overhead, dropping chemicals on the flames, trying to contain the raging beast and reminding me once again how this energy transforms the landscape and everything around us. Flames shot toward the sky, and embers skulked along the ground. It was an eerie sight.

Thanks to the hard work of the men and women who fought diligently, the fire was contained. We were allowed to return home in a couple of days, and the hospital and our homes were unscathed. A cycle of destruction and rage had left the landscape charred and ugly, but a triple rainbow appeared on the day of our return, the first one I had ever seen. The rainbow is an iconic symbol of crossing over and transformation. It is a portal into new life, a promise that the earth will be renewed again and that the circle of life always returns to the beginning.

2009-2012

The town of Whiteriver consists of a post office, a run-down grocery store, and a Burger King. The nearest Walmart is a ninety-mile round trip venture. The isolation drove me crazy. But I was willing to make the sacrifice to help my husband further his career along with the hope in the future we would move down to the Phoenix area where we originally planned.

August 2012

In August we moved into a new home we had built in Estrella Mountain Ranch in Goodyear, Arizona. My husband spends ten days off a month down here with me and the other days in Whiteriver. A lot of husbands do this so their wives can live in more populated areas like Phoenix or Tucson. When his contract expires in November 2013, with most of his loans paid off by Indian Health for living in the remote location, he will decide whether he should stay for another year to pay off the rest of the loans or move down here with me.

I remember the first time I drove through the Salt River Canyon, the route between Phoenix and Whiteriver. I was going to see my husband in December 2009 for the first time at his new location. The beauty of the canyon made me pause. They say life is not measured by the number of breaths we take, but by the moments that take our breath away. When my eyes gazed across the mountains and vistas, I realized I had seen a little slice of heaven here on earth.

My journey to follow the sun seemed endless at times. It took many unexpected twists and turns. But these are my unique experiences that I can call my own woven into my life tapestry. My energy is constantly transforming, moving within the circle of life, moving me toward the beginning and the end. They say everyone is so focused on reaching the destination that they forget to enjoy the journey. It is during that journey that memories are formed, character is built, patience is won, perseverance is achieved, new friends are made, and love is strengthened.

In my journey to follow the sun I have felt the kiss of a desert breeze on my cheek, experienced wonder and excitement when I saw the desert in bloom for the first time, and awed at the delicacy of a cactus flower. And I have beheld the hand of God when he paints across a cobalt blue desert sky in broad strokes of vermillion red, hues of tangerine, and shades of citron, and the mountains turned red in the afterglow.

October 2013

I didn't think my story would end this way, but this truth has just recently become my reality. The years we had endured the poorer and the worse of our relationship had come full circle to the richer and the better. Then suddenly my life spun into another direction with a text from my husband.

In that text he told me I was kindest person he had ever known but that he had never really loved me. That the reason he stayed with me was to help him through school and get where he is now in life. We needed to separate, he said, so he could find his "soul mate" and not die with regret.

This was not the man I knew and loved for the past thirteen years.

My days spun into darkness, but the love and support of family, friends, and neighbors brought me back into the light and the hope for a brighter tomorrow. Accepting the truth is hard, but it does bring peace and the turning point for change.

Some of us are experts in denying ourselves for the sake of others. We get so busy helping other people that we put our own lives on hold. There are no mistakes in life, only lessons, and I have learned to love myself just as much as I love others. I mourn the love I have lost but rejoice in knowing I truly loved, and wherever his life journey takes him I wish him well.

When you commit your life to another person, you create many hopes and dreams. It's hard to see those dreams fade. As you grieve the loss of the future you once envisioned, be encouraged by the fact that new hopes and dreams will eventually come your way. Remember, we are all transforming and evolving within the circle of life, pulling us ever closer into the light of a new beginning. ✍

Biographies

Vincent A. Alascia is the author of *Xristos: Chosen of God, In the Presence of Gods,* and the upcoming novel *Undead Heart.* His work is available on Kindle and paperback, and he has also published online and in anthologies. Originally an East Coast native, he makes his home in the Phoenix, Arizona, area with his wife and three furry felines. He is a librarian by day and an active member of the West Valley Writers Workshop. Find out more at www.vaalascia.com.

Helene Benigno-Stich has written everything from stage plays and novels to short stories and poems, in addition to acting in more than a dozen productions. She also does voiceover work in radio and TV. Helene runs the Young Writers' Academy, which hosts creative writing classes for kids and teens. In her free time Helene continues to work on her next novel, plays tennis, and spends as much time as possible with her wonderful husband, daughter, and cocker spaniel. Get more information about the academy and her writing at helenephx@cox.net or helene@youngwritersacademy.com.

Jen Bielack writes fiction and non-fiction and self-published in 2012 the historical novel *Interrupted Dreams,* an entirely new look at the Titanic tragedy. She is currently working on *Girl Without A Country,* a personal narrative about a Kurdish girl and her family who left Iran for political reasons. Jen divides her time between northern Arizona and New England. Her hobbies include swimming, biking, and pickleball. Hear more from her at Jbielack0714@q.com.

Carmela Ayello Bottita realized her dream to be a writer at the age of sixty. Friends and family loved hearing her stories, and she had many to tell. So she set pen to paper and went for it. In 2012 two of her stories got published; the memoir in this anthology is the third. Now she realizes that a person is never too old to follow a dream, and she hopes to self-publish her first novella by the end of 2013.

Donna Bowring is a short story writer and novelist who lives in Goodyear, Arizona. She has five grown children, grandchildren, and great grandchildren. She received her BA in English from ASU in 1995, attending classes part time while working at ASU in Student Publications. She considers herself almost a native, having lived in Arizona for thirty-eight years. Read her blog at donnabowring. wordpress.com. To contact her by e-mail, go to donnapoet1@aol.com.

Ellen Buikema, writer and educator, received her formal education at the University of Illinois at Chicago and Northeastern Illinois University. Her daughters, Laurel and Julia, provided her training for life. A gypsy at heart, she lives with her husband, Ralph, in Arizona. Hear more from Ellen at ecellenb@yahoo.com.

Heather Cappel is a freelance writer and mixed media artist. She grew up with a sketchbook or a journal always in hand, inspired by the colorful community of aging hippies in her hometown of Eugene, Oregon. She has a BA in English with an emphasis in creative writing from the University of Oregon where she wrote and published poetry. She works as a creative coordinator in the pet industry and cares for an unspeakable number of cats. She currently doodles and scribbles at sketchycorner.com.

John Daleiden is retired from 43 years of teaching language arts in Iowa public schools, the last 24 years in Oskaloosa, Iowa. Currently, he lives in Phoenix, Arizona. John is a member of the Central Phoenix Writing Workshop. His poems have appeared in print journals: *May Dazed: A Cinquain Sequence (2005); Fire Pearls: Short Masterpieces of the Human Heart* (2006); *Atlas Poetica: A Journal of Poetry of Place in Modern English Tanka* (2009); *Ribbons: Journal of the Tanka Society of America* (2013); *Twisted Nightmares* (2013).

His poems also have appeared in numerous online journals including: *Lynx: A Journal for Linking Poets; Sketchbook: A Journal for Eastern and Western Short Forms; Cyclamens and Swords.* John is the co-editor of "Catching the Moment: An International Monthly Kukai," a haiku competition, which can be found at http:// rita-odeh.blogspot.com/. Reach John at daleidenj@yahoo.com.

Bob Duckles has spent his career examining what brings out the best in people at work and how people bring out the best in organizations. He has traveled to distant parts of the world, wandered off the beaten path, found adventure, friendship, and tastes to savor, and collected and made up stories along the way. He now writes those stories in Phoenix, Arizona, where he lives with his lover of 30 years and two dogs, Luna and Maya. Find out more about Bob's work at: www.duckles-international.com or on his blog, "Bringing Out the Best at Work" at bobduckles. blogspot.com. Contact him at bob@duckles.org.

Matt Estrada, a practicing nuclear medicine technologist for more than two decades, has been a fan of fiction for most of his life. He currently blogs for *Advance Medical* magazine (www.advanceweb. com) in their "Radiation Oncology and Medical Imaging" department. He has a near completed novel, which is the first of a trilogy. Matt is a member of the West Valley Writers Workshop. He resides in Peoria, Arizona, with his son, two dogs, and two cats. Find out more about Matt at mattestrada@yahoo.com.

Colleen Grady grew up in Seattle, Washington. At an early age, she enjoyed creative dramatics and creative writing classes. She loved the freedom to mix fact and fantasy. That delight remains today. Colleen is passionate about travel, adventure, photos, and friendship. A degree in psychology complements her curiosity about human behavior, colorful characters, and relationships. Her work history includes extensive public speaking. A background in the travel industry and human services fuels her storytelling verbally and on paper.

A resident of Avondale, Arizona, she is a member of the West Valley Writer's Workshop and the West Valley Writer's Critique Group. At 65, "Desert Oasis," included in this anthology, is her first published story. She can be reached at cdgrady@aol.com.

Dawn Gunn lives in Phoenix, Arizona, with her husband, son, three dogs, and two birds: an Indian ringneck parakeet and a blue-and-gold macaw. While she still has one child at home, her three adult daughters have left the nest.

Dawn is a veteran and also a national board-certified elementary teacher who feels passionate about teaching and animal advocacy. She loves science and tries to integrate it into her lessons, having taught from kindergarten through fifth grades. She is currently working on her high school certification and believes in overcoming adversities through faith, prayer, and mental and physical fitness. Dawn works out daily and runs 5Ks with her family to stay connected and have fun. One of her greatest joys is helping others meet their life goals. She lives by the "no excuses" rule and loves to check things off her bucket list. Talk to Dawn at haphom@live.com.

Donna Hamill was born in Phoenix, Arizona, amidst creosote and palo verde, and her accent—a precious gift from her Southern mother—is one of many surprises. She feels as if she was "born 200 years too late" and for many years struggled to "fit in." She completed a B.S. in math and M.Ed. in Education and spent 15 years at a non-profit, satisfied she was making a difference. Now she is retired and spends time on a low desert farm. She enjoys her heirloom garden that uses seeds from local Native Americans as well as raising heritage turkeys and dairy goats. There are old ways to relearn, like home-canning, cheese making, and sour dough starters, along with a diary to write and share. For the first time, she feels as if she belongs. Donna can be reached at dkh2345@aol.com.

Eveline Horelle Dailey paints when a canvas calls for it and weaves when the rhythm of the loom demands attention. Writing is what she does because she has to.

Her first language of French brings texture to her prose and fervor for the possible. The challenge is often to give shape in English to the songs of her passion. Her inspirations come from nature and people; they are the source of the colors she feels, and they give birth to the distinct complexion of her writing style.

She is read internationally and continues her endeavors as a public speaker, writer, philanthropist, painter, and weaver. She has received multiple awards and is a member of various associations of writers. Find her at: www.evelinenow.com.

Elizabeth Kral graduated *magna cum laude* with her BA in communications from the University of Wisconsin-Parkside and attended the University of Akron Law School. Her early career in public relations, sales, marketing, and business development honed her technical writing and editing skills. She retired after twenty-three years in defense industry management and decided it was time to fulfill her desire to write fiction. Additionally, she thought it was time to leave the Midwest winters of Canton, Ohio, and now spends that season in Surprise, Arizona.

Recently, Elizabeth discovered the lively artist community of Steamboat Springs, Colorado, where she is spending her second summer writing a historical fiction novel, studying creative writing, and receiving encouragement from co-members of the Steamboat Springs Arts Council Writer's Workshop. In Arizona, she is a member of the West Valley Writer's Workshop. Follow Elizabeth Kral on Twitter, Wattpad, and Facebook, or contact her via email: elizkral@gmail.com.

Gale Leach had a number of careers, including teacher, American Sign Language interpreter, technical writer and editor, and owner of a desktop publishing/graphic design business, before she finally achieved a life-long dream: to be an author. When she and her husband moved to Arizona, she fell in love with pickleball, a wonderful sport with a silly name. Her first book, *The Art of Pickleball*, won the Arizona Book Award in 2007. The success of that book spurred Gale to try fiction, something she'd always wanted to do. Her first novel, *Bruce and the Road to Courage*, a heroic fantasy for children, was published in 2011 Bruce's adventures continued in two more books published in 2012, and a fourth was just published in 2013. Writing fiction is now a passion, along with singing and playing Celtic music. Gale lives with her husband, two dogs, and three cats. Learn more about her at www.galeleach.com.

Justin Loyd is a writer living in Phoenix, Arizona. He comes from a working-class family in the Midwest. Justin earned a B.S. in anthropology and sociology from a small college in Illinois where he was defensive back on the football team. With musical aspirations, Justin cut his teeth as a teenager playing guitar and bass in nightclubs around Wisconsin and Illinois.

His interest in nature, religion, culture, and society comes through in his writing, which has been described as "stream of consciousness." Justin's writing is influenced by Jack Kerouac and George Orwell. He is working on his debut novel with a tentative publication date set for spring 2014. Reach Justin at jdahl24@gmail.com.

Jessie Swierski lives in Phoenix, Arizona, with her husband, Mike, and two daughters, Alysa and Kayla. Jessie earned a master's degree in elementary education from Northern Arizona University. She is an elementary reading specialist and a master teacher. She enjoys writing in the modern adult romance, young adult, and science fiction genres. Her hobbies include cheering on the Arizona Diamondbacks, learning vegan recipes, and helping with youth activities at church as well as singing, hiking, and learning about natural healing and medicinal plants. Her passion is spending time with her family. She also enjoys encouraging other people to pursue their passions. Jessie lives the five Fs: faith, family, friends, forgiveness, and fun. Find out more about Jessie at jmswierski@yahoo.com.

Jan Toland has lived in Arizona for more than thirty years. She taught for the Bureau of Indian Affairs, Fort Defiance Agency, on the Navajo Reservation for six years. While there she gained a lifelong love for Native American art. Her collection includes cradleboards, paintings, pottery, and Hopi Kachinas. Today she lives and writes on a five-acre desert ranch in Tonopah, Arizona, with her husband, Paul and her Belgian Malinois, Maya. Jan can be reached at Jtoland34019@gmail.com.

Rita Toma was the fourth of eleven children born in Canada, and some of the responsibility of taking care of her younger siblings belonged to her. Throughout her teen and adult life, she was surrounded by roommates, her own family with three children, and responsibilities that deferred her goal to be a writer. It was always "someday."

At age fifty-six and with dual citizenship, an opportunity arose to live and work in the Valley of the Sun, Phoenix, Arizona. One year later she followed her dream. Four years later she graduated from the advanced writing course at the Institute of Children's Literature. She is currently working on yet another rewrite of her YA paranormal book while enjoying the company and devouring the knowledge of fellow writers of the Avondale Inkslingers. Find out more about Rita at ritatoma20@gmail.com.

Rachel Wallis grew up in a farm and ranch community in New Mexico, the youngest in a blended family with ten older brothers and sisters. As a child she followed the wheat harvest from Texas to Canada every summer with her family and their fleet of trucks and combines. An honor student throughout grade and high school, she completed her college education by attending night classes at Eastern New Mexico University while working full time as an executive secretary. In her late twenties, she traded her steno pad for a forty-year career as a realtor in three states: Colorado, New Mexico, and Arizona. She loves breeding and training young quarter horses and paints, caring for her American Staffordshire dogs, and enjoying her grandchildren and great grandchildren. A novice writer, Rachel draws from life experiences to write memoirs of life in the Southwest. She may be contacted at azkmyra@cox.net.

Dori Williams aspires to be a storyteller who provokes emotion and anticipation within the reader with every turn of the page. Nicholas Sparks, author of *The Notebook,* serves as her inspiration.

Her poems "The Gift," a tribute to our military, and "Child of My Heart," a devotion to her foster children, can be found on

Biographies

Voicesnet.com. She wrote and produced a video presentation, "The Gift," for cable access channel 25 in Racine, Wisconsin. She is a published author, poet, public speaker, and graphic designer.

Currently Dori is writing a series beginning with *Follow Your Heart.* The series traces the journey of Katie O'Brien, beginning in the 1950s, through her full circle of unusual life experiences. Each book in the series weaves her unique life tapestry with threads of sadness, love, adventure, and overcoming insurmountable odds. Talk to Dori at pixelit0@yahoo.com.